My African Safari

My African Safari

Kim L. Capehart

Pentland Press, Inc.
England•USA•Scotland

PUBLISHED BY PENTLAND PRESS, INC.
5122 Bur Oak Circle, Raleigh, North Carolina 27612
United States of America
(919)782-0281

ISBN: 1-57197-165-3
Library of Congress Catalog Card Number 99-070088

Printed in the United States of America

Dedicated to my loving and supportive parents, Dr. William and Sandra Capehart.

Foreword

Before you continue to read, I would like for you to keep several things in mind. Many of these things have come to me while writing this book and some have come afterwards. I think if you keep some of these things in mind as you read, it will help put your frame of mind parallel to my frame of mind, if that makes any sense to you. A friend of mine and fellow colleague Mr. Wayne Hughart has made me aware that this would help make an easier read. I appreciate his input and would like to address them now.

Do me a favor, after reading this foreword, please close your eyes. Picture yourself in an environment like none that you have been or imagined. You stand in a place where nothing is familiar. You could yell and scream for someone you know for a lifetime and no one would hear or come. You could call and it would take them days to weeks to get to you. You are watching people of different lives, beliefs, cultures, and ideals. Are you considered, "predator or prey?" Or are you amongst friends? Do they look to you as help or a treat to their way of life? I must admit it may not be this dramatic but it is a totally different world. One could experience similar experiences right here in the States. For example, someone that has lived in the confines of a small city of couple thousand people in West Virginia and moving to the most extreme parts of New York City or Los Angeles where there are several millions of people. Not only would one be in shock of the pure mass of people present but the pace of life, the lifestyles that come with being in a larger city is totally different.

While reading this book please remember that this trip was totally a volunteer mission. Many countries of Africa and other parts of the world need volunteers and don't get them. Ghana is in one of those categories. I went to Ghana on a volunteer medical internship and as you will read, it was a life changing experience. "Did my trip change their lifestyles, save the people from poverty, and change their way of life?" And the answer is without any question, No. "Did my volunteering help them?" I would like to say yes but can't say that for sure. "Did I have to do any medical/dental treatment while I was there?" And again, the answer is No!

I am trying to take time here to answer some questions that I had and that you might have at the conclusion of reading my book. I say at the conclusion because you obviously won't have any questions before you read this thick massive book. Just kidding, this is very quick and easy reading book. I originally had over two hundred pages but thought I hate reading books that take me more than a few days. So I trimmed it down to the size you are reading now. But with the decrease in size, I did have to eliminate some details that you might be interested in. So it was an arduous task to decide but I decided to cut down the size and sacrifice some detail.

My purpose of volunteering was to help the people as much as I could. They had no expectations of me. Some medical treatment I gave was because I wanted to not because I had to. To be quite honest, with the exception of one or two times, I basically just did the protocol they did to follow up on sicknesses. Since I had minimal training I knew I didn't know everything and didn't act like I did. I knew that they had been treating this for years so I just did as they did for most things. My purpose wasn't to be the savior to the Ghanian people and revive the population with miracle medical/dental treatments. I was just a student volunteering in Africa, just as my friend Amy

Young in Kenya. The treatments I gave, such as delivering a baby, wasn't necessary. They could have delivered it without me, I just happened to be there and witnessed something spectacular that I will always remember. Nothing I did or could have done will ever be necessary for the survival of the population. They have been there for millions of years without me and medical treatment and will be around for another million years without medical treatment. So please keep in mind, I was just a volunteer. If I weren't there they would have still delivered the baby and treated the patients the exact same way and the population would survive.

I hope that this background information will help you as you read and to better help you understand the book. Also, I suggest you read this foreword again after you read the book to see if you come to the same conclusion as I have. I want you to gain valuable knowledge as to how this wonderful country and continent has survived and will continue to survive for an infinite amount of years to come.

Ghana

Map of Ghana: you can see the different regions. I volunteered in the Volta Region. It was about a two hour car ride from Ho in an area called Anfoega. Anfoega is three hours from the capital of Accra.

Acknowledgments

I would like to take this time to thank the people that made this trip possible. First of all, I would like to thank my parents and my family. I think that family is very critical in my pursuit of just about anything, especially when preparing to go to a new and foreign part of the world. I think it would be difficult for anyone to succeed. I feel family facilitates many advantageous characteristics that are the infrastructures behind each individual. I am no exception—my family has infiltrated into me many important and beneficial attributes that have molded me today. They have given me support, let me deal with responsibilities, and helped me develop important morals and values that, for better or worse, make me what I am today. Between you and me, I think I am a better individual because of my family, but I may not be the best person to ask this question. I tip my hat to those that have had to live without the support of their families and continue to succeed, but I know I am a much better person for having mine. Thanks, Mom and Dad, for everything that you have done for me.

I would also like to thank my mother and the employees at her West Virginia flower shop, the Flower Nook. It never occurred to me to write a book about my experiences in Ghana and Africa. Without these women's input and push, I would never have written this book.

They persuaded me that my stories of the trip were very interesting and that most would find them educational and interesting. The Flower Nook also gave me writing pens and balloons that the children loved, and I distributed them to the schoolchildren within the community I lived in.

Finally, I would like to thank West Virginia University School of Dentistry for giving me toothbrushes to distribute to the people in Ghana. Once again, to all of you involved in this memorable trip, I would like to say thank you—especially for your support of and donations toward my wild and crazy endeavors.

Introduction

I would like to take this time to address the background and purpose of the book. I am writing this book to edify and entertain whoever wants to read about the way people in real African countries like Ghana live. With the recent tragedies in Kenya and Tanzania (On 7 August 1998 there were terrorist bombings. The two countries were Nairobi, Kenya and Dar es Salaam, Tanzania. The terrorist act on the U.S. Embassies killed more than 200 people, including twelve U.S. Government employees and injured thousands.), I feel more compelled to write this book. Having experienced firsthand how a tribe in Africa lives, I feel what I am about to write epitomizes the majority of African cultures in Ghana. Even though I haven't visited the rest of the continent, I feel that Ghana is a good marker and very representative of much of the continent of Africa. I won't lie to you—I had my own images of what to expect in Africa but got much more than I anticipated. I based my hypothesis or theory on television stories and books. I imagined that Africa was a very poverty-stricken continent with limited resources. Even with these limited resources, I couldn't speculate with certainty that I knew exactly how poor it was or if modernization had transformed this mysterious continent into a developed continent.

Following are some questions I had in my mind before going on this trip. Are there such emaciating circumstances that carnage of the government and economy is so prevalent that can be translated into poverty? In the upcoming twenty-first century, could poverty be so overwhelming that plumbing, electricity, clean water, and other everyday conveniences are needed? Are these basic privileges an axiom throughout the world? In a world where some have multiple cars, phones, houses, six-and-seven-digit salaries, could there really be a place where finding new clothes, clean food, and water would be an arduous task? I know I only visited one country in this vast land, but I feel that Ghana is very representative of how people in a Third World country live. Even with these predetermined blueprints of Africa, I tried to keep an open mind about what to expect. Let me reiterate, since I had never been to Africa, I only had what television and books offered and didn't know if they represented how things are today. I know that these and many other questions have been answered as a result of my trip and want to share my findings and experiences with you.

I went to Africa on a volunteer medical internship in the summer of 1998 wanting to experience all that Africa's customs and people had to offer. I had longed to go to Africa since I was an adolescent and was very anxious to finally go. The animals, rituals, and remnants of a continent that has been through many tribulations all increased my desire to visit this vast land. I also wanted to see how the continent was coping with the post-slavery, post-European domination. Most of these countries gained their independence only forty to fifty years ago and have many obstacles to overcome in order to catch up with the rest of the world. I visited Ghana, which gained its independence from Great Britain in 1957. I wanted to see a young and developing country that is trying to play catch-up to everyone else, which is the reason I didn't choose developed countries such as Egypt or South Africa. These countries are too established and modernized for the experiences I wanted. I didn't want a tourism experience. I knew the prolific amount of tourism in these countries and didn't think I would experience everyday life. In the following pages, I have summarized my experiences to the best of my ability. I kept a journal so I would have accurate information to tell when I got back to the States. I take direct quotes from the journal throughout this book. Since I haven't gotten direct permission to utilize actual names, people will remain incognito.

Before I continue, let me give you a brief synopsis of Ghana. Ghana is located in West Africa and borders the Gulf of Guinea. On its perimeter are the countries Ivory Coast and Togo. Ghana is a medieval African kingdom in present-day West Mali, with Accra, accounting for over 800,000 people, as the capital. The total population is around twelve million people, with the major cities including Accra, Kumasi, and Ho. Kumasi is the center of the great Ashanti Empire and is the location of one of three Ghanaian Universities. The major currency in Ghana is the cedi (2,300 cedis are equivalent to one American dollar). In the past, Ghana was known as the Golden Coast for its grave amount and exportation of gold. It is also famous for being a major slave trading center in the mid-to-late 1800s. Along the coast, especially in the city of Cape Coast, there are more than seventy castles built by the Western world to use for storage and as docks for slave trading. Today Ghana is known for its historic castles, Lake Volta (the largest man-made lake in the world), and its major export, coconut.

All of the stories are based on events that actually occurred, no matter how unbelievable they might sound. I can't even believe some things that I experienced, but that is why I am telling this story. If my experiences were mondane, then you wouldn't be reading and I wouldn't have written this book, right? If experiences of running from local wildlife, hunting, the Ghanaian health care system, weird and unusual food, and losing my bungalow, toilet paper, crutches, and soap within the first couple of days sound interesting and entertaining, by all means keep reading. I hope you find this book both entertaining and educational. After the trip to Ghana, I am more appreciative of America much more than I was before. I hope that my experiences benefit you in some aspect of how you visualize Africa and Third World countries like Ghana. I also hope to stimulate your mind to think of your present situation and the difficulties these people face. I hope you become more thankful for what you have and do not worry so much about what you don't have. I have some pictures that I hope will give you visual as well as mental images of what I am writing about. When I first looked at the pictures, I noticed one thing, everyone smiles. Even with the situations that they lived in, they were always happy and upbeat about everything. Rarely did I see someone down about anything. I think this attitude is common throughout the continent. I really hope you enjoy the pictures and stories. Enjoy!

Seth: he was instrumental in my survival in Ghana. He and I still communicate via letters and I hope we stay in touch.

Chapter 1

Going To Africa

"Last call for flight 1898, Columbus, Ohio, to Philadelphia, Pennsylvania," the airline representative's voice echoed through the microphone. As those words resonated through my ears, I knew that the journey of my life to the magnificent and mysterious continent was about to unfold. I exchanged good luck and good-bye sympathies with my parents as I boarded the plane. If I had known what was in store for me on this journey beforehand, I might have changed my mind about going to Africa. As it was I didn't know or trust any fortune tellers, so I figured the only way to experience new and exciting places was to go and get my hands dirty. So that is exactly what I did—I was on my way to Africa. As I mentioned earlier, I had wanted to go to Africa for many years, and since I had the opportunity and the time, I wasn't about to let this once-in-a-lifetime experience pass by. My friends all said that I was young so it wasn't too imperative for me to go right away. They were right—and I realized that I had a lifetime to go—but I don't know what is in store for me in my life, so I didn't want to waste any golden opportunities. After all, it was very fortuitous for me to go. Let me explain.

My friend, Amy Young, a medical student at the University of Louisville, found an organization that sponsors students to go to Africa as volunteer medical interns. She and I were so excited to find a program that allows health professional students to live in Africa and gain valuable medical experience. While gaining these new experiences, I was going to go to the continent that I had wanted to visit, so this was a win-win situation. I couldn't believe how perfect this scenario was turning out for me. I thought I was heading to Africa until I checked the school calendar and discovered that the first week of the program and the last week of school overlapped. My perfect scenario turned into a big flop. I was so disappointed that I couldn't go and that my friend would have to go without me. I felt down for several weeks. I finally got over the disappointment and realized that I couldn't go. To keep my time, I would try to find a job for the summer. After applying unsuccessfully for several jobs related to the medical field, I went to the university tutoring service to apply to tutor undergraduates in subjects ranging from biology and chemistry to physics and mathematics. I tutored in these subjects during my undergraduate years, so I knew that I could do this job. After filling out the job application, I found a magazine on the adjacent table and was curious as to its contents.

Then destiny came knocking again, almost five months after the initial disappointment. I found another organization that sends student health professional volunteers to Africa. I was so elated that I rushed home and called the phone number listed. I found out that the dates fit my school schedule, and most importantly, confirmed that the opportunity was in Africa. I immediately called home and told my parents. They had some apprehensions but supported me one hundred percent. I filled out the application, got the letters of recommendation, and waited to hear if I was accepted into the program. After the telephone interview, I was accepted into the program and found myself in the process of going to Africa. I immediately applied for my passport and visa and got all the necessary immunizations for the trip to a Third World country. I should tell you that you should apply for the passport and visa as soon as you can. They can take weeks to a couple of months.

Before I go on, let me tell you about the shots necessary for a trip to a Third World country. Let me be up front with you, they are painful and plentiful. To be honest, I hate shots. I don't mind giving shots, but receiving them is another story. Anyway, one should check with a physician before ever leaving on this kind of a trip. The shots that I received were as follows: a yellow fever vaccination, needed for my visa into Ghana; larium, for malaria; a hepatitis A vaccination, important if one stays long or lives in a poor or uncertain sanitation setting like I did; a hepatitis B shot, needed if one is going to be in contact with blood; a meningococcal vaccination, for meningitis; a one-time polio booster; and a typhoid shot, for adventurous eaters and travelers. Other shots are available, such as immunizations against rabies and cholera. I must warn that these shots are very expensive, ranging anywhere from four to six hundred dollars. But most shots last for many years, and one shouldn't need them again for quite some time. So if one plans on traveling on a regular basis, he or she won't need these shots again for many years. Check with a doctor on the effectiveness of each immunization. Please don't take this as a definitive list of the shots necessary, please check with a physician with knowledge of travel to other countries.

After recovering from the shots, I began to research the country I was to live in and visit. As I stated earlier, I chose Ghana instead of South Africa, or Egypt because of their commercialization and tourism. I wanted to really experience African culture, its people, and all that is encompassed within these parameters. What other African country is less known than Ghana? I don't mean any disrespect of Ghana, but it isn't widely known like other countries in Africa. As I told family, friends, and colleagues of the trip to Ghana, they all replied, "Where?" When I heard that, I knew this was the country in which to experience everyday African life. I had my plane ticket, passport, visa, sense of adventure, enthusiasm, and readiness to take off to another world. I was finally going to Africa.

After boarding the plane and settling down, I met a woman named Lisa. She was very skinny and wore very tight and revealing clothing. These are the '90s, so I really didn't think anything of it. I also noticed her rustic voice, leading me to suspect that she smoked. She was very friendly, and we got to know each other very well. After all, being in a confined area for a seven-hour flight, one talks to and learns a lot about the other individuals. I found out that she was from California. She told me that she loved the freedoms of California. I also found out that she was a Hollywood stripper and a prostitute. I was shocked and interested at the same time. The first question I could think of was, "Have you been with celebrities?"

"Not any famous celebrities," she replied.

I was upset that she didn't have anything exciting to tell me, but I continued to ask questions. Being from West Virginia, I must live Hollywood lifestyles vicariously through others. She did add that she had friends that had been with celebrities but wouldn't negotiate any names. After dinner she drank several bottles of complimentary alcoholic beverages and soon fell asleep. As I tried to fall asleep, I thought that if this woman was a harbinger of things to come, I was in for a real adventure. After arriving in Amsterdam, the Netherlands, seven hours later, I had a day layover, so I collected my baggage and looked for the hotel bus. The first thing I noticed was that the taxis were Mercedes-Benzes. As it turned out, I had just missed the bus that takes people to the hotel, and it only ran hourly. So I decided to get into a taxi and go to the hotel. The taxi driver was very friendly, but he did exhibit hostility towards Americans. He told me that he thought they were arrogant and snobbish, but he also mentioned that he would live in America if he had the opportunity. I don't know if it is jealousy, but it seems like this is the axiom for the way most of the Dutch view America and Americans. I also noticed some wooden shoes in the airport stores. A few people wore them. I thought that was neat and also thought the shoes must be very uncomfortable. Anyway, after a two-mile trip, the total cost was thirty-four guilders (Dutch money). When converted to U.S. currency, that sum equals around seventeen dollars (two guilders equal one U.S. dollar). Yes, it cost almost eighteen dollars for a two-mile trip. I immediately learned that taxis are very expensive in Amsterdam, and that I should have taken a bus. This experience made me think I should take more care so I did not go broke before I even reached my destination. After all, I'm in new and unfamiliar countries so I am targeted to be taken advantage of.

After checking in and settling down, I called home. My mother answered the phone and told me that it was three o'clock in the morning. The time difference between Amsterdam and the East Coast was seven hours. After resting and calling home, I got onto a bus and toured downtown Amsterdam. Yes, I got on a bus—I guess this old dog learned a new trick. After I arrived downtown, the bus driver suggested that I take a boat tour of the entire city. He told me it was worth my time and didn't require too much money, so I rode on a small boat that runs through the city. It was very beautiful, and I was glad that I came downtown instead of napping.

After the boat tour, I walked through the streets and entered a coffee store, thinking I could get a snack. What I found out was that coffee shops in Holland don't have any snacks, or at least this coffee shop didn't. In fact, it didn't even have coffee. It was a hash house. There was a lot of marijuana, and there were many marijuana accessories. I didn't realize that hash is legal in the Netherlands. Needless to say, I left and continued my tour. As I walked I read a sign that said I was in the red-light district.

I perused the stores from the street and noticed women of all ages, shapes, and sizes standing in the windows for all to see. They were all wearing teddies, and after closer examination I realized they weren't mannequins. My curiosity got the better of me, and I walked into a store and asked for the manager. I knew what it was but wanted to confirm what I imagined. I asked the manager, "What do these women do?" He told me that they would do everything, and I replied, "ooohhhh." I then asked him for prices, and he told me that it depended on how old they were. He continued to tell me that an older woman would cost forty to fifty guilders, and a younger woman would cost between 250 and 300 guilders per hour. The manager then asked me which lady I would like for the hour. I replied, "No thanks." He was very persistent. I made up many excuses, but to no avail. I finally told him I was a student and had no money. I guess this satisfied him, because he told me thanks and let me go without another sales pitch. I was then satisfied with the information I gathered and quickly realized that the last bus ran in fifteen minutes, so I left for the bus stop.

I was totally amazed that marijuana and prostitution are legal. Being a future health care provider, I also thought of diseases. I thought of some friends back home who would love to live here, with marijuana and prostitution both being legal. After returning to the hotel, I ate a club sandwich and fries for dinner. After dinner I found only one English-language channel, so the television experience was limited. When the program concluded around midnight, I too went to bed.

It was eight o'clock in the morning, and I tried to wake up. As I do at home, I hit the snooze button several times. I finally woke up at nine o'clock and got ready to eat breakfast. As I headed down to the hotel restaurant, I noticed cleaning equipment from the night before next to my door. I wondered how things run with cleaning supplies in the main hallway. After I arrived at the restaurant, the waiter asked me for the room number to which to charge the breakfast. I forgot mine and had to go back to the front desk to ask for the right number. I guess this is indicative of my forgetfulness.

Immediately after sitting down, I met two girls. Their names were Barbra and Kate, and they had just completed month-long study abroad experiences in Spain. The two ladies were very nice and thoughtful and noticed that I was eating alone and invited me to join them. They were from North Dakota and were majoring in Spanish at the University of North Dakota. They related to me some of their experiences in Spain and said they enjoyed their time there. Barbra said they hated living in hostels for a prolonged amount of time but soon got used to sharing with everyone. Kate told me she had learned more Spanish in one month than she had in two years at the university. I figured I would learn the native language very quickly in Africa, because I would be forced to speak it all the time. They also told me that their visit coincided with the Running of the Bulls. I was glad to know that they kept up on world events. We talked about the Protestant-Catholic conflict in Drumcee, Northern Ireland, and in Belfast. The two girls are also ardent soccer fans and spoke of the World Cup. We spoke for about an hour and then said good-bye. After saying good-bye, I checked out and headed for the airport on the hotel bus. Another eight-hour plane trip, and I would finally arrive in Accra, the capital Ghana and a new world.

Chapter 2

Touchdown in Africa

On the connecting flight between Amsterdam and Accra, I met some very nice and interesting people originally from Ghana. The first individual was a priest and his name was Philip. The second individual I met was a woman who was a hairdresser named Mya. And the last person I met was a man who was a graduate student at the University of Ghana in Legon and his name was Raaja. I did notice that none of them presently live in Ghana.

Even though the plane was at capacity, they speculated that over ninety-nine percent of the Ghanaians were just visiting. Most were fortunate enough to get visas and didn't plan on returning to live. Like the rest of the people on the plane, the three individuals were all visiting. They were all fortunate to obtain visas to their respective countries. The priest was from Dallas, Texas; the hairdresser was from the province of British Columbia in Canada; and the graduate student was from the University of Michigan. All lived in Ghana in their youths but have found better lives outside of their native country. Besides living outside Ghana, the second significant thing that I noticed was how friendly the people were. I know I asked a million questions about Ghana and the region in which I was to reside. My kind and helpful acquaintances answered everything with an explanation, for which I was very grateful.

Philip, the priest, was going back to visit his old church for two months. He said that he missed his homeland but was glad that he is in America. He told me that Catholicism is the prominent denomination in Ghana, especially in the Volta region, the region I was to live. He was very nice. Since he lived in America, he knew what comparisons were relevant for me when I arrived in Ghana. He told me that not all of Ghana has electricity, and that most of the country doesn't have plumbing. I figured as much but kind of hoped that I was wrong. He also told me that even in the capital of Accra, electricity only runs on shifts. There is currently a power shortage in Ghana, so electricity is conserved.

In May 1998, U.S. President Bill Clinton visited Ghana and promised the country that the U.S. will supply more than sixty million dollars in funding for another dam. Only one dam supplied the entire country with electricity, and in the dry season, there is an electrical shortage. President Clinton promised Ghana's President Rawling the U.S. would help build another dam for the country. His visit to Ghana is the first by any American president, so needless to say the Ghanaians almost think he is some kind of savior. His visit alone raised the morale and dreams of the entire country and strengthened its belief that Ghana too will be wealthy in the future. It is also seated firmly in Ghanaian heads that the U.S. is very kind and generous. I hope that the U.S. follows through on its promise to Ghana and builds a new dam. I know what people in some other parts of the world think of the U.S. and would hate for them to hold the same opinion as the taxi driver in Amsterdam. I personally know they need the dam and would appreciate it more than anyone could imagine.

Anyway, the priest told me to always dress in dress pants and have them ironed, because Ghanaians, especially in Accra, think very poorly of people in shorts or wrinkled slacks. I thought this was weird but was prepared to deal with it. Mya, the hairdresser was from Vancouver, and she was going home because her mother had passed away. Since communication is slow, she got the message several weeks after her death. She was very kind, even when she was in so much pain. I tried to limit my questions to the other two since she was in mourning, but she loved answering questions for me, so I did ask her a few.

She told me that her mother and her tribe saved for many years to obtain enough money to send her to Canada. She got a visa because she was doing missionary work, which helps in ascertaining a visa. Ever since she started to work in Vancouver, she had sent more than twenty-five percent of her paychecks back to her tribe. She said that she missed her family and friends. She also wished everyone could come with her. I asked her how she dealt with coming to the Western world and what she thought about the people and culture of North America.

She said, "I had a hard time adjusting because I didn't know what many things were and how to use them." She had problems with the microwave, computer, telephone, and refrigerator. She then went on to tell me that the people were not very nice, and that many were very rude. "I cried and wanted to go back home when I first got here," she said. She told me that the people and the land were so big and very unsupportive. But with hard work and determination, she worked as a maid and saved enough to go to cosmetology school and become a hairdresser. Now that she has made it, she loves North America and wishes all her loved ones back home could experience what she has experienced. She also added that since being around the people more, she realizes that the people weren't that bad—she just wasn't used to the way the society operates. She said, "Everyone in Ghana is laid-back with no time constraints . . ." She later added, "Here in Canada, time is very, very important, and that causes a lot of stress." I thought she was very open-minded to think this way and not keep her original notion that Canadians were all rude.

Raaja, the graduate student at Michigan was an exchange student from the University of Ghana at Legon. His status as a student enabled him to get his visa to the U.S. He asked me how long it took me to get a visa to Ghana. I told him about three days, and he was stunned. I asked him how long it took for him to get a U.S. visa. He explained to me that several thousand people apply for visas to the U.S. every month, and only one or two get one. I was amazed and asked, "Why is it so hard?" He said the Ghanaians won't come back, and the U.S. is very strict because of that problem. I started to realize how hard it is to get to America. Many people are willing to leave everything behind for just a chance for a different and perhaps better life. I asked if he was going to go back to Ghana after his education and he grinned and said, "What do you think?" From that grin and the comment, I knew the answer.

Eight hours had passed, and we were about to land in Accra. For the past two hours I had seen nothing but white from the land below. I assumed that it was the Great Sahara Desert. I hoped to visit it before I returned home. After I talked to everyone for what seemed like days, they were ready to pass out, and we all fell asleep until we landed in Accra around nine o'clock at night local time. The moment I got off the plane, the heat and humidity almost knocked me down. I had never felt anything like it before and immediately began to perspire. I walked down the stairs to the ground. The airport was about two hundred yards away, so I had to walk to the building to get my luggage and go through customs.

After the short hike, I finally entered the airport, and it wasn't too bad. It wasn't air-conditioned but had lights. When I got inside, I looked for my representatives but couldn't find them. I started to get worried and asked an airport employee where I could find them. He told me that they were probably outside, because civilians are not allowed into the airport unless they are flying in or out. He helped me go through immigration and customs and to get my passport stamped.

After I got my luggage, he took me outside and I was shocked to find hundreds of people in a circle waiting for passengers coming out of the airport. I was also puzzled that four or five men were helping him pull one piece of luggage on wheels. I thought, "How nice." After I found the representatives to help me, they took me to a taxi. At this time, the "nice" men carrying my luggage were going to charge me for it. They all screamed and pressured me into giving them money. I kept telling them I had no money to give, but they were persistent and aggressive. The people there to pick me up told me to give no money, and they tried to tell them that I wouldn't. They all spoke either Ga or Twi, so I had no idea what they were saying. I could tell that they were arguing because they were yelling at each other. I was a bit flustered after getting in the taxi, but we finally started to leave the airport. The representatives, Sandy and Paige, told me that the airport workers and taxi drivers were the only ones who would harass me for money. I was relieved but didn't believe her completely.

It was dark, and I couldn't see much of Accra, so I would have to wait until morning to see what an African capital had to offer. Boy was I in for a shock. We first stopped by a restaurant, and they ordered me dinner and bottled water. My first Ghanaian dinner was rice with chicken. As we rode toward the hotel, Sandy told me that I would stay in one of Ghana's best hotels. It had breakfast, lights, and running water—which made it elite in Ghana. Lights and running water are both limited.

I was very excited that I wouldn't have to stay in a dirty hotel room for the night. After arriving, I was again shocked at the conditions of this first-class Ghanaian hotel. It had one room with a bed and a small desk. There was a community bathroom with a tub, sink, and toilet, but only the tub worked. The bathroom served four rooms, but since tourism isn't great in Ghana, I was the only one to utilize the bathroom.

That first night, I realized how hot it is in Africa. With no air conditioning and only a window with no air movement, it got very hot, very fast. I sweated profusely but really didn't want to take any clothing off, because ants were prominent in the room. There weren't too many of them, but there were more than I was accustomed to back home. I couldn't believe how bad, in comparison with home, the hotel room was. I did realize that this was a great and expensive hotel by Ghanaian standards. The citizens couldn't afford to stay there. I was starting to get worried— if this was the best they had to offer, and I was to be a three-hour car drive away, how much less could there be?

Hotel at Ho: this is a picture of the first rate hotel room I stayed my first night in Ghana in Accra. I must admit, during my first few nights in the tribe, I was begging to be back in this room.

It took me awhile to fall asleep. I dozed off by convincing myself that these were the worst conditions Ghana had to offer, and that it couldn't get much worse. So I fell asleep, and breakfast came at seven o'clock. Breakfast was hot tea and eggs on bread, with some kind of red vegetable mixed in the eggs. I ate it because the chicken from the previous night wasn't too good, so I was hungry. The red stuff wasn't very tasty either, but I ate the egg sandwich anyway.

Sandy and Paige said they would be by around nine o'clock for my language lessons and currency exchange, so after eating I went back to sleep. Seven o'clock in the morning is no time to be up to just be up. I woke up again at half past eight and started to get ready. I prepared to take a shower and tried to turn on the water. There was one problem—no water came out of the shower. I then recognized a large trash can with a lid. I lifted the lid and saw water and a bowl. I wondered what it could be, and then it hit me that it was to be my bath water. I then started to worry again, wondering if this was the best Ghana had to offer—and it wasn't even close to what I am used to in the States. I continued to take a bath and finished after thirty minutes. It took me a long time to get the shampoo out of my hair, because I didn't have enough pressure to rinse the shampoo totally out. So instead of using the bowl to rinse my hair, I dipped my head inside the trash can. After brushing my teeth and getting dressed, I was ready by nine.

Unfortunately, Sandy and Paige weren't. I soon learned that Africans have no sense of time. They have no deadlines, and time means very little to them. I had to learn this custom very quickly, because I am very punctual and hate for people to be late. Waiting for the women to come, I sat in the Jacuzzi-like conditions in the hotel room for more than two hours. Finally, they arrived with no contrition for their tardiness. I was mad that they were late and that they didn't apologize for their tardiness, but I realized this was the way they lived.

After entering the daylight for the first time, I noticed few owned cars. I saw many cars, but they were taxis or tro-tros or belonged to upper government employees. I know this because the two women told me. I also saw some very modern cars and was told that these belonged to the U.S. citizens that live in Accra. Sandy and Paige also explained to me that one can't buy a new car in Ghana very easily. Most of the newer cars are imported by the person wanting the car. But most don't have money to purchase new cars, so there isn't a high demand for many new car lots. They told me that most of the taxis and tro-tros were used cars over ten years of age. I know now what happens to cars that we use and then no longer want. They are sold to Third World countries, or at least Ghana. So rarely would one find a car less than ten years old. The majority of the cars that I noticed were Datsuns for taxis and Volkswagen vans for the tro-tros. Since few own cars in Ghana, I traveled in taxis and tro-tros the majority of the time.

Let me explain what a tro-tro is in comparison to a taxi. A tro-tro is a bus that continuously picks up many people along the way to a certain destination, whereas taxis take one to two people. Tro-tros are much cheaper than taxis, especially since taxi drivers try to charge outrageous rates to foreigners.

Ghanaians refer to all foreigners as "white people." I learned another valuable lesson— that "white people" doesn't include just white-skinned people, but every ethnic group outside of Africans. I am from South Korea, and I was called "white man" even though I have dark skin. I thought that was very fascinating. They also think that whites automatically have money and will try to exploit them. I couldn't believe how much they tried to cheat people who didn't know what they were doing. Let me give you a prime example. I motioned for a taxi driver to stop and asked him how much it would cost to go to the University of Ghana from Accra. He told me fifteen thousand cedis, which equals around six dollars. I then had Paige ask the same driver the price, and she was told five hundred cedis, which equals about twenty to twenty-five cents.

After learning how to negotiate with the taxi and tro-tro drivers, I was confident enough to go out on my own and negotiate fair and reasonable prices. The Ghanaian "art of negotiation" is essential for anyone outside the area to learn and master. Those who don't will lose big not only on money, but on their belongings.

There is a lot of pickpocketing in Accra, so people have to watch it when others bump into them. They should also watch out for the children begging for money. They will take whatever they can. Most of the begging children are aliens from a nearby country, Chad. I wanted to give money to the children, but Paige said that I shouldn't because it could be dangerous. The children's parents watch to see who gives them money and harass them for more later. "You feel sorry for them but can't afford to give to every child and also don't want to put your life in danger," she said to deter me from giving money, so I didn't.

Sandy and Paige also warned me of some local customs that I needed to know. I already knew about wearing nicely pressed clothes, but there were a few more things that they said I needed to know. First of all, I should not use my left hand for anything. They said, "Don't use it to wave, or give money, or anything." I asked why, and she told me that it is very rude, and that I might get yelled at for doing so. Sandy told me that since most people are right-handed, many have the idea that most use their left hand to clean after defecation. I thanked them for the warning.

I wanted to see how true this warning was, and I soon learned not to use my left hand for anything. When buying bottled water, I handed the money to salesperson with my left hand. He immediately gave the money back and took the water away from me. He said something in the Ga language, so I had no idea what—but I figured it wasn't anything good about me. Sandy also warned me to say *Mede kuku* after everything I say to anyone, out of respect. *Mede kuku* means "thank-you" in Ewe, and after the left-hand experience, I didn't test this custom to see a native's reaction.

Downtown Accra: you can see the cars and people during the late afternoon.

After I had seen most of Accra, I was amazed at how primitive the capital was in comparison to home. But the capital is very modern in comparison to where I was heading. One thing I noticed was a reservoir running along the roads. I first thought it was for drainage of rainwater but soon remembered it doesn't rain enough for the implementation of such a system. I then realized the weird odor I smelled since I arrived wasn't the atmosphere. It was the natural bodily wastes. This system also made me realize how Accra was trying to modernize with a sewage system. There were telephones, but they were not readily available.

If one wants to use the phone, one has to go to a communication center. At these centers one can call internationally or locally. Most local businesses have phones, but they cannot call out of the local area. So finding a phone, even in the capital, was an arduous task. There were gas stations, businesses, banks, cars, paved roads, and many other luxu-

Government buildings: construction and art museum in the capital of Accra.

ries in Accra. I was astonished to see a Shell gas station and also Coca-Cola everywhere in Accra.

One quick thing about Coca-Cola in Accra. I bought a bottle of Coke and drank it. Nothing unusual, right? I was ready to throw the bottle away, until I was told that I had to return it to the person I purchased it from. I asked why, and they told me, "You didn't buy the bottle!"

I was very confused and exclaimed, "Yes I did."

The person then said, "No you didn't, you bought the fluid but not the bottle . . ." If I wanted the bottle, I would have to pay for it. I thought he was joking but immediately realized that he wasn't. So I gave the bottle back to the clerk.

I then continued to tour the city. As I perused the town, I noticed that in the nice buildings are American or European companies. By nice, I mean they have electricity twenty-four hours a day, because they have generators, phones, and air conditioning. But most businesses and residents don't have these luxuries. After registering my passport and visa at the U.S. Embassy, we headed to the bank. The banking facilities are air-conditioned and in a very structurally sound building. I exchanged two hundred dollars and later learned that this amount would have lasted for several years in Ghana. When I gave the bank teller the traveler's checks, she stared at me for a few seconds and said, "I have to go get more money." Evidently they didn't have that much money, because two hundred dollars is equivalent to about many years' salary for an average Ghanaian. Not many people need that much money in one lump sum.

I had learned the "art of negotiation" with transportation and gotten some local currency, so I was ready for my language lesson with William at the University of Ghana. (This is the same university that the graduate student on the plane attended.) William was a student there, and he showed me the campus before we got started. The campus is among trees, and the region is very tropical. It is a very beautiful campus. The buildings lack technology and modernization, but it is a good university with many programs and schools. They have an undergraduate program with a wide array of degrees to choose from. They also have a graduate school to get a master's degree.

Dental, medical, and law programs are all offered at the school. The facilities and books for the medical, dental, and law were well below standard. Most books were outdated, and their availability was scarce. The dental school only had five chairs for students to gain experience on patients. The technology was also very archaic. Needless to say, outside the major Ghanaian cities, the dentist is an extractor without local anesthesia. Even within the major cities, extractions are prevalent over restorative care. But with the absence of candy and a lot of sugar, most Ghanaians have healthy, white teeth. The books offered to dental and medical students were very poor and outdated. They knew nothing of new advances and discoveries. This lack of updated learning tools made me wonder about the level of health care in Ghana. William told me only the top Ghanaian students can go to medical or dental school. Most complete high school and can enter the respective programs when they finish high school.

Ghana is an English-speaking country, but different local dialects prevail everywhere. Some of the local languages are Ga, Twi, and Ewe. Ewe is named after the coastal Ewe, who are mostly traders and fishermen found in this region. Ewe is spoken in several regions and is a tonal language. Tonal means that different words can be brought about with tonal differences. It is spoken in the Volta region of Ghana, in Togo, and in the eastern region of Dahomey. The alphabet has thirty characters—twenty-three consonants and seven vowels. All the English letters except *c, j* and *q* are present. In addition, there are six Ewe letters that aren't in the English alphabet. The digraphs that most foreigners find difficult to pronounce are *ts, tsy, dz, kp, gb,* and *ny.* After a couple of hours of lessons, I felt comfortable with basic greetings and sentences I might encounter with patients. I was now ready to head off to Anfoega Catholic Hospital in the Volta region.

Leaving wasn't as easy as it seemed. A hospital employee, Seth, a person I got to know very well, picked me up, and we waited on our ride to go to Anfoega from Accra. The person was to have the vehicle ready for us to leave at five o'clock. Once again, the Ghanaian time schedule was in effect. We sat and waited for over a hour and a half for him to arrive. I was hot and very relieved that our ride had arrived. The vehicle was a jeep that looked like it was ready to go to the junk yard. It was the typical jeep seen in movies and television shows. I was afraid that it wouldn't make it, and that we would be stranded in the middle of the forest. Outside of Accra, the paved road turned into trails of dirt and weeds. I couldn't believe that we were going to ride more than three hours through the jungle.

Southern Ghana is very tropical, and the northern region is very arid. I must admit that during the bumpy ride, I really enjoyed the environment. The trees and hills combined with the lakes and streams made truly beautiful sites to witness. I tried to spot wildlife throughout my trip but was unsuccessful to seeing anything major during the first two hours. I did see some cockatiels, parrots, and other exotic birds. I also witnessed some vultures feasting on something from a distance. The vultures are really big and awesome to watch eating. It is also spectacular to see them fly, because they leave big shadows on the landscape below. Not all vultures are of great size, but these were very large, and their large shadows were embroidered along the hillsides.

I really enjoyed the sightseeing part of the journey until we abruptly halted. A huge gorilla-like animal stood in the middle of the pathway. I couldn't believe what I saw. I don't know if it was a gorilla or a related species, but it stood about two-and-one-half to three meters tall and was a spectacular sight. Since the animal wasn't going to move, we had to drive very slowly and carefully around it. As we drove by the creature, I stared into its eyes and it into mine. I can't explain it, but I felt in awe and feared for my life at the same time. As we drove away, the creature watched us until I couldn't see it anymore. I asked Seth if this was common to see, and he said no. He had only seen a couple his entire life. He told me that I had seen something that most Ghanaians don't see. I was very happy and grew more at ease with the trip to the countryside.

As we traveled through the path, I got to see the real African society. With the exception of them running around naked, I found it exactly as I imagined it and similar to what was displayed on television. The poverty is overwhelming. I felt so sad for the people. The little huts with straw roofs and mud walls were very depressing. One could see how each tribe was separated from one another by a couple of hundred yards. At each tribe, women and children walked up to us to see if we wanted to trade for or buy food or water. Most of the villages don't use currency, but some do, because a visit to Accra or another major city requires money. At each village, the inhabitants offered many items: water, crackers, bread, grass cutters on a stick, birds, water, and whatever else they could find. Some villagers sold drums, clothing, and jewelry. At these villages, one could watch people making the items. With the exception of a few items, most of the materials were available in the wild. I couldn't believe how skilled the workers are. They use stones for hammers and chisel wooden nails if they have no nails available.

Along the way, I spoke some Ewe and tried to speak some French with them. Good thing I paid attention during my two years of studying French—not. I could barely understand some of them. The French dialect was muffled in with the native Ewe, so I was usually lost. Ironically, I could understand them speak in Ewe much easier than in French—two years of studying French, and I can't understand a word, but I can better understand a language I studied for a few hours. I did talk to someone that spoke French without the Ewe accent, and I could understand that person better. So I guess I did learn more than I thought in college. Some of the natives also spoke Swahili, as they do in the eastern part of Africa, but not many. The individuals that spoke Swahili were from Kenya and the eastern coast of Africa. Anyway, villages with people selling and trading were numerous for most of the trip.

After the bumpy three-hour ride and surviving the wildlife, we finally reached the hospital. I couldn't believe a hospital would be located in this region. There were no roads, no vehicles of any kind, no telephones, and no electricity. The hospital serves more than eight tribes, each tribe averaging two to four hundred people. So the hospital was available to around two thousand people. I was pleased to see that the bungalow I was to stay at was an actual building and not one of the huts I had seen for the past three hours. There was actually a car in the bottom of the bungalow, so I thought I was in luck. After walking in and meeting all the hospital employees, as well as the hospital administrator, Mr. Dankmer, I evaluated the bungalow. It had no modern conveniences, but it wasn't too bad. There were lots of insects, small mammals, and reptiles running through the bungalow, but I could deal with it. I was very pleased with the housing and thought I had it made. After seeing huts for several hours, I got worried. Seth was a hospital employee and also a tribe member in the region. So he, as well as other employees, lived in the villages. Only Mr. Dankmer and the volunteers lived at the hospital, aside from the patients. My room wasn't great, but I could deal with it and thought I could handle living in the bungalow. I later found out that there was a van at the hospital, but neither it nor the car below my place worked. The van had no engine, and the car also needed some work. So I had some anxiety over the fact that I had no transportation and that I was over one hundred miles away from Accra.

Mr. Dankmer told me that two other people volunteered at the hospital. One, Melanie, was from Canada, and the other, Marissa, was from Holland. Melanie wanted to become a hospital administrator, and Marissa was going into accounting. Since Seth was the hospital accountant, Marissa worked with him. Melanie worked with Mr. Dankmer.

After meeting and greeting everyone, I learned that there were no doctors on staff at this hospital. I couldn't believe this dilemma. The previous doctor left a few months earlier, and they had been trying unsuccessfully to recruit a new permanent doctor. I was the only person knowledgeable about medicine within the hospital, and I had only completed my first year of dental school. This frightened me tremendously. The nurses were somewhat knowledgeable but didn't know too much. After all, most were trained by watching other nurses over the years, so it was kind of like the blind leading the blind. Few trained nurses worked at the hospital. A Ghanaian doctor who didn't work at the hospital came by every so often. Having many areas needing medical help, the Ghanaian doctor traveled. I soon learned that they were depending on me to have knowledge of how to treat many tropical diseases. I had studied some tropical medicine and parasitology, but I was not nearly competent enough to diagnose and treat patients. I did take tropical medicine, general surgery, and pharmacology books with me to help me if I needed them. Bringing those books was the smartest thing I could have ever done, as I soon learned.

When I had settled in and begun to see patients, I became more comfortable with treating them. I knew that as long as I didn't try anything too drastic, I would be fine. By drastic, I thought surgeries (with the exception of suturing cuts) and combining medicines that were contra-indicated. Harmful drug combinations were very common, and many people were becoming sick and even dying because the nurses didn't know what drugs interact nega-tively. That is where bringing the drug book helped. I hadn't had pharmacology in school yet, but knew that this book would help.

I was really enjoying my first exposure to the patients. But during the first day of work at the hospital, I noticed smoke outside the building near my bungalow. I rushed out and realized my place was burning, so I immediately ran over to get my stuff out with the help of Seth. I did get my things out in time, but the bungalow continued to burn. I couldn't believe that my place was gone. What was I going to do since that was the only bungalow?

Chapter 3

Everyday Life as a Tribe Man

Since the fire decimated my bungalow, I had the difficult task of finding a new place to stay or going home. I was on the verge of going home until Seth invited me to stay with his tribe for the remainder of my internship. I hesitated to stay within the confines of the tribes but didn't want to go home. So that evening I moved my belongings to the village. I wanted to take some pictures of the hut and the interior of the village, but I wasn't allowed to. I was a bit confused because they told me they did not want people to see that they lived in these conditions, and I said that they shouldn't be ashamed of how they live. They did not view it with the same perspective I did, so I took no pictures of the huts. I was told that many foreigners take pictures and then sell them for handsome profits when they return home. They did, however, let me take some pictures at the community center, and some pictures of hospital employees and patients.

I took some good pictures of the people, patients, community center, and Accra, as well as my friend Seth. Without him, I would have been lost throughout my entire stay in Ghana. He was so friendly and stayed with me until I was on a plane to go back home. I couldn't believe how nice and friendly he and his tribe's members were. They did everything for me and wouldn't let me do anything. They cooked, did my laundry, and did anything else that I needed. I tried to do some of the chores, but they insisted that I was "gracious enough to come to their country and volunteer," so they should take care of me. I felt uncomfortable for a few days but soon got used to it. I soon discerned that this kindness is evident throughout the country.

Before I continue, let me explain the conditions around the village and within the neighborhood. I will also tell you about my experiences with the wildlife in the area. I described earlier the conditions of the huts on my journey to the Volta region—I found many similarities between those villages and these. First of all, the walls are usually made of clay or mud, but some are wooden and plaster. The plaster and wooden walls are few and far between, and only the chiefs and other nobilities live in these nicer huts. The majority live in the mud and clay huts with straw roofs, and sometimes there are no roofs present at all. Seth lived in a clay hut with a straw roof, and the floors are made of dirt. He lived with his mother, father, and sister, so there were a total of four in the family. They were all very nice and very generous for letting me stay in their homes and live off food they hunted and gathered. Surrounding each tribe is a tropical jungle that defines the separation between the different tribes. The distance between tribes is no more than a couple of hundred meters.

While staying with the tribe, I saw a wide array of animals. To this day I still have no idea to what family or species they belong. For instance, there are animals the natives call "grass cutters." As I mentioned, I have no idea what species these grass cutters belong to. They have long, rigid, protruded noses they use to cut through grass. Other animals that I saw were snakes, spiders, ants, crickets, monkeys, sheep, chicken, and a plethora of mosquitoes. The Lake Volta region is renowned for the mosquitoes. These mosquitoes are carriers of the parasitic infection malaria. In the evenings, I recall them being so abundant that I could swipe my hand through the air and have several of them in my palm. After a couple of days, my arms and legs were swollen from mosquito and spider bites. Thank goodness I took some antibiotics that reduced the swelling, or I might have been in grave trouble. The swelling decreased, I was back to normal in about a day, and it never came back.

There were many mosquitoes, but there were almost as many spiders in hidden places. Some of the spiders I saw had to equal the size of a quarter in diameter. I won't lie— snakes and spiders are two things that petrify me to death. To give an idea of how scared I am of snakes, let me flash back to my undergraduate days at Marshall University. I once dropped a vertebrate zoology class purely because we had to study snakes. They were dead, but I still couldn't handle looking at or touching them. Spiders scare me too, but not to the extent that snakes do. Today I am not quite as scared of either of them. I don't want any of them as pets but can tolerate them much better. Seeing spiders everywhere and snakes slithering through the weeds, I have become somewhat more tolerant of their presence.

Since there is nothing anyone can do to inhibit them around people and the houses, I quickly got over the snake dilemma in an expedient manner. I vividly remember standing about five feet from the edge of the weeds and perusing the landscape while dinner was being prepared. Hearing something in the weeds, I looked down and noticed the head of a snake peeping through. Because I was scared of snakes and this was my first encounter with one in the open, I froze. I couldn't move or even talk. I don't know what was wrong—maybe I was in shock, or maybe I was frightened for my life. I was in big trouble. I went numb, was sweating, and couldn't have moved if I wanted to. As I stood there frozen, the snake slowly slithered out of the weeds and onto the village floor. It was about five feet long and looked very scary. Of all the locations for the snake to travel, it crawled about three feet from me. I was so scared that I could have died but was too tense to do that or anything else. As the snake moved past me, a child saw it and yelled for the men to come and kill it. Immediately and with urgency, the men killed the snake. Seth told me that I should have said something, but I explained my fear to him. He couldn't believe that I had such great anxiety that I was unable to yell for help, but he understood. He said that snakes are very common in the area and they try to kill them whenever they spot them. I was relieved they fear snakes too, but they deal with it just a little better than I do. As the days passed, I saw more of them and reacted much better than I initially did. I won't say I can touch a snake, but I can stand to look at them in an aquarium or on television. Snakes were present, but not nearly in the numbers that spiders were. Now that you know my phobias, let me continue my adventure.

My first day in the tribe was an adventure. I woke up to a tribal dance around five o'clock in the morning. I asked if I could take a picture, but they wouldn't let me. I didn't blame them—the ceremony is very awesome and sacred to witness. Some men drummed and others danced, while the women prepared breakfast before the morning hunt. I felt very privileged to witness such a ritual. I asked Seth what the dances and drums meant, and he said, "We do this every day except Sunday . . ." He then added, "Doing this daily ritual keeps our spirits high and also keeps us prepared for what life has to offer." In other words, it is similar to the military marches and drills soldiers do to prepare and stay sharp and ready for anything.

He also told me that each kind of drum signifies a different reaction when going to war. For instance, the drum I purchased and brought home is called a Bor-Bor-Bor, which in Ewe means to "bend down." So among all the different drums playing, a trained tribesman knows to bend down when he hears the sound of this particular drum. This is very crucial in battle, for the drum is pivotal in tribal warfare. I like to think I have a pretty good ear for music, but I couldn't distinguish between the different drums. I then understood how trained the men are and how important the drums are in African societies.

Upon the completion of the ritual, it was time for prayer. They spoke in Ewe, so in the beginning I was clueless as to what they were saying. But as time progressed, I was able to pick up on the language and became a little more fluent. The ritual and the prayer lasted for almost an hour, and then breakfast was ready. The sun slowly rose— a sign to go hunting. They tried to go early so the heat would not be too bad. As they left to hunt, I left for the hospital. After a nine-to-ten-hour day, I returned to the hut.

I was shocked to find my crutches disassembled. I had decided not to take them that day in order to exercise my legs. I have a medical condition called arthrogryposis, which is a congenital genetic disorder that affects most of the major synovial joints, especially in the lower limbs. Exercise is good therapy for the joints and muscles to keep them from getting stiff. Anyway, I walked into Seth's hut and saw my crutches taken apart. I wondered who and why anyone would disassemble them. I asked Seth's father, Greg, "What happened to my crutches?"

He replied, "We took them apart."

That was obvious, and I asked, "Why?"

Greg said that the chief was afraid that the crutches were weapons. They have crutches at the hospital, but not aluminum, as mine were. So they were unsure of the material and thought the crutches had possible other uses. I just laughed and asked if they were satisfied to know that they were just crutches. He said that they found nothing and would put them back together. Needless to say, reassembling them wouldn't put them back in their original state. They wiggled too much for me to use, so I gave them to the hospital to use for patients. They had no crutches so even this wobbly pair was of some benefit. Mr. Dankmer was very appreciative of my donation. They had wooden crutches, but one was broken, so these aluminum ones would be hard to break. They annealed the wobbly parts over an open fire and made the crutches much stiffer.

During the first night after eating dinner, I wanted to take a bath but changed my mind after they told me the only water they had came from the same source from which they took their drinking water, and in which they did their laundry and sometimes relieved themselves. The thought that they used the same water source for all these was too much for me to handle. At the bungalow, I had clean water from a small waterfall behind the hospital. But the water at the tribe is too dirty to bathe in. The lake is also in the open, so everyone sees everyone bathe. I am a modest person and found this difficult too. I know this sounds disgusting, but I didn't bathe in that water for four or five days. I just couldn't bathe in the filth, but I finally broke down and washed in the lake.

After a few days of doing so, I learned not to worry about my modesty and not so much about the dirty water. How could I do that? Remember, I was in the middle of nowhere, with *no* clean water, *no* phones, and *no* cars, so I knew I had to bathe very soon. If I did not, I could have caught many diseases from having dirty, clogged pores. The smell could also get very bad. I knew the lake was dirty, but I used soap and shampoo, and it was better than not bathing for weeks and weeks.

I also learned that nudity isn't a big deal to the citizens. During the day they wore very nice, clean, ironed clothes. But at night, it isn't unusual to see people peal off the clothing. The heat is very intense, and this relieves some of the heat while they sleep. In case you are wondering, I didn't take my clothes off except to bathe. I just couldn't go that far with the nudity. I bet you are wondering, as I did, how they iron their clothes. I got to see the women heat two metal plates and lay clothing in between them. To my astonishment, they looked very pressed—not like they would if they had been taken to a dry cleaner, but this method was very effective.

Beth and baby Jennifer: I took this in late afternoon behind the hospital. You can see that she is getting prepared for the evening hours since her clothes were slowly coming off.

As the evening progressed, I had to defecate. I learned another important custom. When one has to defecate, he or she goes out into the woods, digs a hole, and does his or her business. That wasn't too bad, but I was afraid of the wildlife while my bare butt was exposed. I was about to go when I noticed my toilet paper was missing. I had brought several rolls to last many weeks, and they were all gone. I asked Greg about them, and he said that the chief had them. I asked him why. He told me that the entire village could use the toilet paper, so he took it. I went to the chief and asked if I could use a roll.

The chief was very friendly and said, "Of course, any time."

I didn't say a word. I got a roll and started off into the weeds. As I walked, I thought, "I'm borrowing my own toilet paper—what is wrong with this picture?" I then decided not to say anything and just let them use it. With this in mind, one of the first Ewe sentences I learned was "*Afikae affoegee nay fey day*?" which translates, "Where is the toilet paper?" I thought that I was in their country and their village and should not do anything to upset them. I was puzzled that they didn't take my CD-Walkman or my camera but took the toilet paper. Then I thought, "What are they going to play on the Walkman and where are they going to develop the film?" Western valuables are worthless to them, but basic necessity items like toilet paper are priceless. I thought that was very interesting. From then on, they always let me get a roll, as long as I returned it. They were always friendly when I asked if I could borrow one. I look back on this and find it very amusing.

After dealing with the "toilet paper dilemma," I was tired and wanted to go to bed. The previous night I had only slept about an hour before the tribal dance. One reason I had trouble sleeping was the fact I slept with the entire family. They don't have bedrooms or even beds, just large straw mats with blankets over them on the ground. We all slept in the same bed, and it was very uncomfortable. The heat, insects, and rodents were unbearable. During the night I could feel spiders and mice crawling over me and mosquitoes biting me. These factors were enough to keep me awake and afraid to sleep. So I was hoping to get some shut-eye that night, even though I had the same anxieties. I still did not get any sleep. I kept thinking of the wildlife and constantly brushed creatures off of me. The others didn't mind the animals because they were used to them. Of course, I wasn't and didn't think I would ever get over my anxiety so I could get some sleep. As it turned out, it took me four days to finally fall asleep and get a good night's rest. I was tired for a couple of days, but the lack of sleep finally caught up with me, and I did not think of the animals. Unfortunately, I never did get used to them, but my mind did adjust so I could bear with the wildlife. My body was also telling me I needed sleep immediately.

After I got used to sleeping and bathing, I needed a new adventure. I took a day off from the hospital and told the administrator I would make it up on Saturday. On my day off, I decided to go hunting with the tribesmen. If you knew me at all, you would know I am the farthest thing from a hunter. I had never been hunting but thought it would be a fun and new experience. After breakfast, I prepared to go. I didn't take any weapons because I didn't want to hurt anyone, especially myself. The men use bows and arrows, sharp rocks, javelins, and sticks to hunt for their meals. The types of animals they hunt vary depending on the season. While I was there, they hunted monkeys, wart hogs, grass cutters, snakes, and anything else they could kill.

After about three hours of being out in the jungle, I was dead tired and wanted to go back but couldn't once I had started. As I was standing and leaning on a tree, I was hit by a monkey. I shouldn't say "hit," but it landed on my head and quickly jumped into the tree. I couldn't believe that a monkey was momentarily on my head. I quickly ran away from the tree, looked up, and saw the monkey eating something. I felt around and made sure I hadn't gotten cut. I told Seth, and he said that happens a lot.

Unfortunately, the hunters didn't catch anything major, just enough for lunch. They usually try to catch enough for lunch and dinner. If they do, they don't have to hunt in the afternoon for dinner. But they had a new, inexperienced, and loud hunter with them—me. I made way too much noise, and they told me that I wouldn't be allowed to go hunting again. I was not too disappointed, because I hate hunting and was very tired. I am glad that I did go once, because I learned how skilled these hunters and gathers are. They could sneak up on a deer and sit on it in the States. This shows just how good they are, but one has to remember that this is how they survive.

If they don't catch food, they starve. They don't have a McDonald's or a grocery store where they can pick up Big Macs or chicken. The situation reminded me of studying history in high school, when we learned how the early colonial population hunted for and gathered food to survive. I can't imagine myself having to hunt and collect food in order to eat. I have a hard time going to the grocery store to restock. I know I couldn't survive if I had to work hard for my meals. The skill these men and women have is amazing. They may not have the modern-day conveniences that we are accustomed to, but they deal with the deficiency and survive. I really admire the skills the Ghanaian people have in order to live day to day. Since I was kindly banned from hunting, I let them hunt and continued to work at the hospital. I feel more comfortable in the health arena than in the hunting arena.

Before I continue, I want to spend some time talking about the women and their duties, as the men go hunting. I have to give credit where credit is due. These women are the hardest working people I have ever seen. They constantly work and rarely have a chance to rest. They are up before the men to begin cooking breakfast and up later than the men cleaning. I couldn't believe how much work the women do. They are the infrastructure to the village's existence.

Let me describe a typical day in the life of a tribal woman in Ghana. It is before five o'clock, and the women are up preparing breakfast. If the animals aren't dead, they kill them and then cook the food. A typical breakfast has to be large enough for a several hundred people, so it takes a lot of food and the effort of many people to prepare any meal. The women are just as skilled in their duties as the men are in theirs. While the men take part in the rituals, the women kill, clean, and cook the food. They also have to start the fire and take care of the children. Let me also describe how they handle a crying baby. Back in the States, if one hears a crying baby, one checks on them. In Ghana, they let them cry and cry. This method of child rearing must work, because only the youngest babies cry. The other infants do not cry very often.

Seeing the women start a fire is amazing. I watched one woman start a fire, and she had a flame started within five minutes. To this day I still have no idea how she started the fire. She showed me, and I tried but couldn't get a flame started. It usually takes the women a hour and a half to have everything ready to eat. It comes just in time, since the dancing stops almost in conjunction with the food being completed.

The food is served in a unique way. They have bowls, instruments to cook with, and utensils to eat with, but there are not enough utensils and plates for everyone to have his or her own. In order to feed everyone at the same time, the women cook the food in bowls and then put it in a big bowl. The bowl is big enough for several humans to sit around comfortably. Everyone walks up and grabs the food out of the gigantic bowl. Everyone feeds out of the same source. Every meal is served in this manner.

When the food has been served and the men have eaten and gone hunting, the women begin the cleanup process. They not only wash the bowls and other cooking instruments, but they clean the village and the clothes. They also take care of the children. After cleaning and checking on the children, the women put the babies on their backs with sheets and collect fruits.

Living in a tropical region allows them to have an abundance of fruit. The women collect mandarins, bananas, and coconuts in baskets and carry them on their heads. Believe me, there are many types of bananas. I watched them women carry large and very heavy baskets and bowls on their heads. I tried to carry a little thing on my head and dumped the contents everywhere. (Are you getting the idea that I couldn't survive here for very long? I know I was.)

After collecting the fruits, the women return to the village, and the men are back with food for lunch and dinner, if they have had a good hunting day. While the men rest, the women go through the process of preparation and cooking again, another two-hour extravaganza. Once eating and cleaning are completed, the men go hunting if they didn't catch enough for dinner. While the men are away, the women usually collect more fruits or fish to help in collecting for dinner. Sometimes they collect enough to sell or trade to another village, or in rare instances, tourists. They go fishing with the children nearby, teaching them some of the tricks in collecting good fruit or in fishing without scaring the other fish away. After fishing or collecting fruit, they usually return to the village and begin to make clothes for the children and the men.

The women usually take a back seat to the children and the men. I don't mean that women are viewed as secondary people or in the background of the men. In the villages, women have the same rights as the men. Equality between the men and the women is evident—men help cook, look after the children, or do anything the women ask them to do. There are arguments, but compromise is the usual route followed in order to resolve issues. It seemed to me that they both sacrifice for each other, and mostly for the children. The children are top priority for both the men and the women. I think it is very mature and responsible for them to have such high consideration for their kids. I was very impressed and really admired them for their care of children.

When the women have made as many clothes as possible, the men are usually back with dinner. So it is time for the women to prepare, cook, and distribute the food to the entire village again—another two-hour venture. I don't know about you, but if I had to spend two hours preparing every time I wanted to eat, I would be all bones. I have a hard time putting things in the microwave and pushing some buttons to eat. I don't know how they do this over and over again. I guess in order to survive, people do what they have to do. I just can't say enough how impressed I am with the skills that the men and women have in order to survive. After dinner the women continue to make clothing, and the men usually start to make either drums, guitars, or weapons for the remainder of the evening.

Barbra: she is making soap. You can see some of the conditions of the community center next to the tribe.

While the parents work, the children play. The kids mostly play a game that we call "It." One person is "it" and chases others to tag them, and a tagged person becomes "it." They also play with dull weapons to help develop their skills. The men teach them how to use the weapons, and they play with the older, duller weapons to sharpen their skills for when they get older. These skills are a necessity.

After the kids are worn out and the light is limited for building and sewing, it is time to go to bed. But first, the entire village gets together again for a short prayer. I learned, after gaining knowledge about the language and being able to translate for myself, they were thanking for the day's fruitful hunting and also for the safety of the entire village. They also praised God and Jesus. The country is very religious, and Catholicism is the most prominent religion in this area. Upon completion of the prayers and the good nights, it is time for bed. Bedtime was usually around seven or eight o'clock in the evening. After all, they wake up very early every day and work very hard, so sleep is needed in order to be ready and have their skills at their sharpest for the next day. This is the routine that these villagers follow daily. Variation from it is not common.

I should describe my second brush with death, or at least thought it was. It was on the weekend, because I wasn't volunteering at the hospital. The end of lunch was approaching, and I was going to help clean up when I heard something in the weeds. I immediately thought of snake, but was not the same kind of noise. It was too loud, and there was too much movement in the weeds for it to be a snake. I turned and looked, an a wart hog was running directly at me. I immediately started to run in a zigzag manner so the hog could not build up speed. I think he could have caught me if I didn't zigzag. They are very fast and shouldn't be taken lightly when they do chase a person, although that usually isn't a problem in the States.

I was really scared that this thing was going to plow me over and trample on me. The weird and frightening thing was that the tribe members were laughing. I was running from a hog for my life, and they laughed. I yelled for help, but they continued to laugh. I screamed, "*Help!*" The hog was less than a meter from me when it dropped to the ground. I turned and looked, and I saw a spear was sticking out of its head. I was in awe and scared that whoever threw the spear could have hit me. I looked to see who threw the spear. It was Seth. He was more than ten meters away, and he threw that spear with great accuracy. I was in double shock and needed to recover not only the hog chasing me, but from the spear that flew more than twenty meters away and landed a few feet from me. I quickly asked Seth, "What if you missed and was just a few feet over and hit me?"

He told me, "I would not have hurt you and I am very accurate and rarely miss."

I then asked while taking a deep breath, "Rarely?"

He just laughed and said that they only had to hunt for a few hours that day, since they would use the hog for dinner. I then asked him why everyone was laughing. He told me that this kind of thing happens quite often and that it was very unusual to see someone running in a zigzag manner and screaming at the top of his lungs. I was kind of embarrassed but got over it. I do not get too much practice at home running away from hogs. Now that I think back, it would have been very amusing to see someone running in an odd manner and screaming very loudly. It just happened to be me. I was glad to be the object of their amusement, especially in a society where laughing and fun is invited but not common because of the need to work and survive.

I really enjoyed seeing them laugh and smile. They all loved to have fun, but due to circumstances, fun is a rare commodity to them. Don't get me wrong, they are happy people that smile a lot but fun activities are rare. Since candy and sugar are rare, their teeth are in great shape. Their teeth are white, need very little work, and are in better shape than many at home. Dentistry in the area encompassed no restorative work such as fillings. Minor cavities that would be fixed with restorative dentistry in other areas are corrected with extractions—the first and last option for disposing of a hurting tooth. As I mentioned earlier, the dental school at Legon was not modern in comparison to the West. The school did have restorative care instead of just extractions, but the technology did not enable the dentists to give the quality of care to which we are accustomed. Amalgam restorations were common but composite restorations didn't exist. Before I left for Ghana, I obtained around one hundred toothbrushes from school to give to the villagers around the hospital. I did not know if they use toothbrushes or some other cleaning instruments, but I took them anyway. I was somewhat surprised to find that they use toothbrushes and toothpaste. The toothpaste is Ghanaian, so I don't know if it contains fluoride. I gave the toothbrushes to the hospital billing department to give to patients as they left the hospital. I didn't know any of the people, so the only way I knew to distribute them to as many as possible was to leave them with the billing department. They were very grateful, and I received many thank-yous for giving the toothbrushes to them.

One thing that I enjoyed tremendously was speaking to the schoolchildren about preventive health, and anything else they wanted to know. As we all know, children have very inquisitive minds, and Ghanaian kids are no exception. I would first discuss the importance of washing and maintaining sanitary conditions when eating and after using the bathroom. I know it isn't a big problem for most of us, but in Ghana the conditions are usually very unsanitary. Many infections result from the poor conditions. A lot of the outpatients I saw had intestinal problems linked to eating food that wasn't properly cleaned or was not cleaned at all.

I know they have limited resources with which to clean, but some things can be maintained. Coconuts, mangoes, and other fruits with thick coatings should be very good and clean. Some of the people would collect these fruits, open them, and let them lay for days, so anyone could come and pick one up when he or she wanted to. I saw the convenience but also the possible infections that can and do result from this practice. Another health problem I saw was the practice of them relieving themselves in the lake from which drinking water is taken and where laundry is done. I told them that they should excrete in the fields and weeds and should try to avoid excreting in the water. I said this would not only keep clothes from stinking, but it would also leave cleaner water to drink. Drinking, bathing, and laundry in the lake is a must and can't be avoided, but urinating isn't necessary.

I tried to tell them some fake, disgusting stories of people that I had seen who had problems from drinking water with urine in it to get my message across. I know I should not have lied but didn't think it could hurt. It did work, because I saw fewer people urinating in the lake. In my journal I have written about a kid named Steven who walked up to me and very excitedly said, "*Wee zo Dokta Kim, Medi trade tsilefe tsi, neda godoa,*" which translates roughly into, "Hello Dr. Kim, I haven't used the bathroom in the water [lake] and always do it in the garden [weeds]."

I said, "That's great," and told him to keep up the good work.

He then said, "I like it better in the weeds anyway because I try to hit spiders and insects while I go to the bathroom."

I laughed and told him good luck. Anyway, while I lectured at the school about preventive health issues, I was a little shocked to see that these kids had questions about acquired immune deficiency syndrome (AIDS) and the human immunodeficiency virus (HIV). In the hospital, the government has little posters that stress the importance of picking partners carefully. They didn't know too much about the virus, but I was impressed that they knew that it was serious and deadly. I continued to tell them how the deadly virus is contracted and how to protect themselves from it.

I talked to many students throughout my stay and noticed that they were very receptive and starved for knowledge. I just wish I had books and other tools to give to them, because their eyes lit up when I told them anything. But with the lack of money, supplies were rare, and having recent books was nearly impossible. The students used chalk and chalkboard to turn in assignments, and the teacher had a big chalkboard in each classroom.

There were, if I recall correctly, three classrooms. I spoke to each class during my stay. One classroom was for elementary, or primary, students; the second classroom was for middle school; and the third classroom was the high school, or secondary school. Many children start school when they are five or six, and those who finish are between eighteen and twenty. Not many make it this far in school. I did meet many who finished school and went to one of the Ghanaian Universities. But I also saw people who didn't make it through the system. Those who do usually become elites in Ghanaian society. Since they can enter medical, dental, and law professions directly out of high school, there are very young professionals. I must say, with total respect for Ghana and its universities, I am glad that the U.S. mandates that doctors from Third World countries, whether they be physicians or dentists, take the boards and repeat residencies in order to practice in this country. I know it is because of the limited resources and economy, but the health care system is very archaic and the medical books outdated.

If a student makes it to secondary school, he or she will usually go to college, get a degree, and be very high in the social realm. Being high in the social realm in Ghana is similar to the situation in the U.S.—doctors, dentists, professors, government employees, and teachers are all considered to be very successful and are given much respect by the people. Talking with the people and students, I learned that anyone who can give medical or dental treatment is at the top of the social chain. I was told by some teachers that they are regarded more highly than chiefs and the Ghanaian president in some parts of the country. I thought this was very interesting.

As I went from the middle to the secondary classes, the hospital administrator told me to talk to the people about succeeding with a disability. He told me to tell them that having a disability doesn't mean one needs to quit life and beg for money. In Accra, I saw many disabled people begging on the sides of the streets. I felt sorry for them and initially thought that Ghanaians did not care for the handicapped or acknowledge them. I am glad I talked with Mr. Dankmer, because that is not the case. The country is very accepting and does whatever it can to help. He said, "It is engrained in their heads to quit because they have a disability." He told me to talk to the older group about this matter, because they would understand and appreciate my advice more so than the other children. I concurred and talked to them about living with a disability and dealing with it. I was amazed at how much they had to say about the subject. Evidently this is a big issue in the tribes, because they want everyone to work and not give up. Most feel that giving up and begging for money is very disrespectful not only to the families, but to the entire country.

One student asked, "Can handicapped children succeed like normal children?"

I answered, "Yes, of course!" But I had to remember that these students only knew of handicapped people giving up. Hearing me say that one can succeed and become something was foreign to them. We talked about this issue alone for more than two hours, so I knew this was a very new subject to them and wanted them to learn all they could. After I lectured about the subject, Mr. Dankmer told me that I did a great job, and that many students were inspired to become better ones and try even harder to become successful in any occupation. He said, "The students thought if you, a person with a lifelong disability, could become a dentist, then they should be able to do the same in their life." I won't lie—I felt pretty good about the lecture and was glad I could convince them to become whatever they wanted to be. For the remainder of my stay, students came to me asking questions and seeking advice. I gladly answered them and hope that when I go back to Ghana I see the same people in good and successful careers.

I had gotten to meet everyone in the tribe and was becoming a source of knowledge for both the kids and the parents. On my walks to the hospital and back, anywhere from ten to twenty-five people walked with me and asked questions about me, America, and anything else they could think of. I didn't have the answers for everything but tried to answer what I knew. I must confess that I did get sad when they asked me questions about America, or "Heaven," as they called the U.S. Some evenings after I came home from the hospital and ate dinner, the entire tribe would ask if they could ask me questions about "Heaven." I said yes, and at the beginning there were only thirty to forty people. But as time went by, the entire village was there listening and hanging on to my every word. I could see the dreams and imaginations floating in their eyes as I told them about America.

Here are some of the questions that they asked that made me very sad and more appreciative of what I have: "How do you go to the bathroom?" "How do you catch and prepare your food to eat?" "Do many people have electricity or phones?" "Does everyone have freedom?" And finally, "Do dreams really come true in America?" I answered these questions and many more. I could not believe how quiet the entire tribe got when I spoke. I was also amazed at how much they longed to go to the States and how they would do anything to get there. When I say anything, I do mean anything. Many women proposed marriage to me and offered to be my slave if I would take them with me. I wish I could have taken all of them with me, but I had to say with much contritions, "Sorry, I can't."

Seth said, "Kim, I know slavery is over but if there was a boat at Cape Coast to collect as many people as it could to go to the States to be a slave, everyone would want to go." The questions and Seth's statement made it clear to me that these people don't want to live the way they do. I always thought resistance among the natives contributed to the lack of development. I was dead wrong. Most all the people want change and want it now. They all wish they were like the more developed countries, but they also know they have a lot of work ahead. Since gaining its independence from Britain, the country has made little progress. Mr. Dankmer told me that there are just enough natural resources to generate income for the country to develop at any kind of a pace. He said, "The people want change and would do the work, but when you don't have the economy or the resources, what can you do?" I then understood the problem. Motivation, imagination, and work weren't the problem, there was just nothing to offer to the rest of the world.

I then asked him who built the hospitals and the national theater if the economy was so bad. I thought the Ghanaian government built all the buildings in Accra but was wrong again. He told me that the Ghanaian government built Independence Square, but the national theater was built and donated by either Japan or South Korea. He couldn't remember which one it was. He then went on to tell me that the government didn't even build the hospital—the Roman Catholic Church did, for missionary work. He told me that is the reason Ghana has any hospital to date. There are some Ghanaian-built hospitals, but most of them are a result of missionary work. He also told me that building any major facility in Ghana would require outside help—for instance, the new dam President Clinton promised. This made me think of how generous other countries like South Korea are, and hopefully America too, when it builds the new dam.

Even though the smaller countryside cities are slow in developing, I have to report that I did see growth taking place in some of the major cities. In Accra, I saw a sports arena for football (soccer) and other sporting events in which Ghanaians participate. I also saw construction on new buildings that showed me that growth is trying to overcome conformity with present-day conditions. Growth is seen not only in Accra, but in other major cities of Ghana. Kumasi and Ho are also growing, which I think is very positive and encouraging. All this growth trying to peek through makes me very anxious to see how things will progress in the coming years. Although progress is very slow, it is coming. I have hope and confidence that Ghana will become a modern country, and that fewer will suffer in the countryside.

Chapter 4

Hospital Experiences

Now that I have discussed the everyday activities of the civilians within the community, I would like to expand on the conditions in the hospital that serves and treats the eight surrounding community tribes around Anfoega. Throughout the book, you will see some pictures that show some patients and the wards.

Let me mention one funny thing about the nurses. When I asked them if I could take their pictures, they all quickly volunteered. But the funny part is that they wouldn't let me take a picture unless they looked like they were busy. So before I was allowed to snap a photo, I had to promise to send them a copy of the picture, and that I would take a pictures of them doing different tasks. Right after I took a picture, they stopped pretending to work and usually went to gossip with the other nurses. I thought that was very humorous.

Another incident that I found amusing involved the hospital accountant, who happened to be my friend Seth, and how he took care of hospital money. I watched for several days and noticed that he did not separate the bills or coins and just deposited them into a drawer. I also noticed that he never counted the money at the end of each working day. I finally asked him how he knew how much the hospital made. He told me that he had no idea. He showed me the drawer with the money in it, and I saw that there was no organization of the denominations. He told me that as long as there is money in the drawer at the end of the day, the hospital has made money. He then told me that having money in the drawer is "very, very good." I laughed to myself over this unusual way of maintaining and keeping track of the hospital's money. Mr. Dankmer usually counted the money.

Now that I am finished with my flashback, let me continue to discuss the hospital conditions. I would first like to discuss the physical infrastructure and logistics in place. As you can tell from the pictures, the hospital is like a palace compared to the huts. You might also speculate that even as nice as the hospital is, it can't compare to one in a more civilized and modern country. I worked at Anfoega Catholic Hospital, which is located at Anfoega-Akukome in the Anfoega region in the Kpandu district of the Volta region. I know that is a mouthful, but that is how the regions are described. It resembles our state, city, county system in the States. For example, I went to school at Marshall University, which is in Huntington, West Virginia, in Cabell County. The hospital is under the jurisdiction of the Catholic Diocese of Ho.

In 1959 Dr. Kwame Nkrumah, the first Ghanaian president, opened the hospital. The blueprint encompassed several facilities to accommodate the basic hospital setting in Ghana. The hospital consists of a doctor's and hospital administrator's bungalow, a combination outpatient department and meeting hall, consulting rooms, a laboratory, a supply room and pharmacy, three wards for obstetrics and gynecology, a children's ward, and a medical ward.

The nurses and staff have done a fantastic job in helping as many people as they have. In 1997 the number of patients was significant. Let me explain some of the statistics for the hospital of the 1997 year. Keep in mind that these are strictly estimates, because charts and book work are practically nonexistent. They saw more than eight thousand outpatients, admitted more than one thousand patients, and delivered more than two hundred babies. I will add that there were some minor surgeries, but no major operations because the facilities are inadequate for such tasks. With the limited resources and technology, I think they have done an unbelievable job in maintaining and helping so many.

The most prevalent diseases and conditions are malaria, caused by *Plasmodium falciparum*, and tuberculosis, caused by *Mycobacterium tuberculosis*. Other conditions also exist, such as upper respiratory infections,

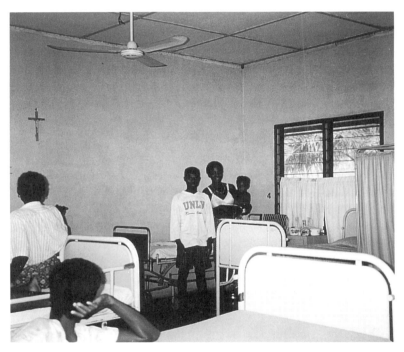

Ward at the Hospital: you can see patients at the hospital. Most had TB or malaria. You can see a ceiling fan above but it didn't work. When the hospital was built, they added many fans and lights in expectations that electricity would soon follow.

hypertension, skin diseases, rheumatic and joint diseases, pregnancy complications, and diarrhea. I also saw a few cases of HIV and AIDS. Carbuncles, typhoid fever, schismaniasis, leishmaniasis (both of which are parasitic diseases found in the area), and other infections were also present within the hospital and community. I cannot emphasize enough the splendid job the nurses do in treating the patients with the hospital's limited and archaic supplies.

They do great for what they have, but the overall health care is not very good. Many die because of the lack of trained personnel, especially doctors. The mixing of drugs, infections, cross-contamination, and many other factors cause many unnecessary deaths. Since few of the staff were properly trained in many medical treatments, and especially drug interaction, I saw many patients die while I was there. I was very shaken at the mass of deaths and the frequency with which they took place. But over time, I learned to deal with several people dying every day.

Death is very common in this part of the world. I saw many families react very little to the deaths of loved ones. While witnessing the lack of emotions from the families, I had to remember that death is very common in Ghana and that the people must be used to loved ones dying. It is not that they do not react because they do not care, but it is because it is so common that they accept it much easier than we do. They realize that death is a natural and frequent part of life. The philosophy is the same at home, but death is less frequent and seems more troublesome to us because the lifespan in the States is much longer than in Ghana. This is why I think they deal with loss of life much better than we do. Witnessing anywhere between five to ten people dying every week, I also began to understand how much easier it was for me to deal with the deaths of villagers. I will add that the almanac says each woman in Ghana averages six births.

I also learned and watched several rituals for burying the dead. The people of this area have a two-day burial ritual, and the ceremonies only take place on Fridays and Saturdays. If someone dies on Sunday, a ceremony never begins until Friday. To be honest, I have no idea why they wait for these designated days, but this is how the ritual works. On Friday, there is a parade with the family members and a band walking through the village. Saturday is the actual day of burial. I saw probably five to ten of these rituals every weekend. It was very depressing for me since very few people close to me have died. I know that I am young and that death of loved ones is inevitable during my lifetime. I just hope I can deal with the loss with the same respect and dignity that Ghanaian villagers do.

Since I was there on a volunteer medical internship, I saw a large number of patients suffering from the illnesses I mentioned earlier this chapter. I won't lie to you—I was way out of my league in treating these kinds of conditions and diseases. First of all, I was still in school. Secondly, I have no experience in treating most tropical diseases. And finally, since tropical diseases are rare in the U.S., schools don't concentrate heavily on them. To make up for my lack of knowledge, I did take precautionary measures. As I mentioned earlier, I brought several books—a pharmacology book for knowledge of drug interactions, a general surgery book, and an emergency medicine book. Even with these, I still lacked the actual experience to deal with and treat these conditions. But remember, I usually did what the nurses did in treating these diseases so I wasn't really necessary for these patients.

I must reiterate at this time that many of the medical personnel at the hospital lacked valuable knowledge and experience. So even with my limited experience and education in these conditions, I knew more than they did and knew what to look for. That enabled me to treat patients better than the personnel at the hospital in some cases. The staff's lack of knowledge scared me at the beginning, but I soon got past the fear and began treatment. I also realized that the only way that I could really hurt patients was with drug interaction. Since I had a drug interactions book, I thought I was relatively safe in this respect.

I basically educated the hospital staff about drug interactions among the limited medications they have. I wrote down all the medicines available at the hospital and told the staff what each does and how it interacts with others. I had paper, and I wrote in Ewe. Writing everything in Ewe helped me tremendously, both in learning about drugs and in learning the language. I tried to impress upon them that these precautions would eliminate many deaths, because they didn't know anything about the drugs. The government, which supplies them, gave them a listing of the drugs and what they do, but it was out-of-date and not detailed enough. The government listing also didn't tell about the dangers and results of mixing drugs.

My educating them about the drugs would save many lives, but I still worried that many people would die because of poor storage methods. The small, single room in which they store the drugs has only one window. It has no electricity, no air conditioning, and no fans to keep the drugs at room temperature. I would guess that the temperature in there was 130 to 140 degrees Fahrenheit. In these conditions, I knew that some drugs lose their properties or become unstable. The sad thing was that there was nothing I or anyone could do about the situation. I did tell them about the problem but didn't harp on the subject because I didn't want to convey all negative comments about hospital practices—especially since they couldn't do anything about this problem. I tried not to tell them how to improve things they couldn't fix. I didn't want to say much, because they have such good and happy lives and I didn't want to keep telling them how things could be better. In other words, I didn't want to depress them about something of which they have no control.

One of my obligations with the internship was to talk to and train the staff on basic procedures like taking blood pressure, counting heartbeats, sterilization, and other procedures. I was very shocked to see that they took blood pressure and counted heartbeats incorrectly. I noticed this when I was seeing patients, and the nurses came and told me the patients' blood pressures and heartbeats per minute. Let me give an example. In order for a patient to be examined in the outpatient clinic, the nurses measure the blood pressure and heart rate. A man came in the examining room, and a nurse told me that his blood pressure was 170 over 210, and that his heart rate was 190 beats per minute. I thought these numbers were way too high. I asked again to make sure I heard her correctly. She repeated the exact same numbers. I asked if she was sure and if all patients had such high numbers, and she said yes.

I immediately gathered all the nursing staff for a meeting session. The purpose of the meeting was to learn how they were taking these measurements and to teach them how to take blood pressure and heart rates correctly. I asked someone to tell me how he or she took the blood pressure. I was shocked at the response. One nurse told me that she got the bottom number in the blood pressure by reading what the instrument says when the patient can't stand the pressure from the cuff anymore. She got the top number from the reading when the nurse decides to let the pressure out of the cuff. I asked if they used a stethoscope to take the blood pressure, and they said that they didn't. They then told me they counted heartbeats by adding the two numbers together and dividing by two. So, in my example above, the sum of 170 plus 210 is 380. Divided by two, that equals 190 beats per minute.

I was astonished to learn that this was how they had done things for many years. Even though they took the blood pressure, they still didn't know what the numbers meant. They take readings because the government requires them to. I couldn't help but giggle some, because it was hard to believe that this was how they had done things. I didn't tell them they were doing things wrong but told them how they could get better results. I didn't want to hurt their feelings, so I tried not to say things like, "You're doing this wrong," or, "Don't do it that way." But I did say things like, "Let me show you a better way," or, "To get better results you should do . . ." In order to explain it to them, I told them the normal range of numbers. I then told them how to do these procedures. I actually took everyone's blood pressure and let everyone take mine using the blood pressure cuff with the stethoscope. After I taught them and let them practice on each other, they realized how wrong their old methods were. I think they then realized how I tried not to put them down, because they all gave me big hugs and thanked me for being so nice to them.

After teaching them that numbers like 120 over 80 are more normal than 170 over 210 for the blood pressure, I quickly showed them how to measure heart rates. Seeing their thirst for knowledge and interest in learning saddened me, because I saw how bright these people are. They are willing to learn but can't because of the economic situation and the substandard educational system.

Now that I have described the hospital conditions and training of the personnel, I will talk about some of my interactions with patients during my internship. First I will relate an experience I will never forget. It was about half past three in the morning, and I was sound asleep. I was abruptly awakened by a woman screaming. I had heard people scream during the middle of the night throughout my stay, so I did not think anything of it and tried to go back to sleep. Several minutes later, I heard Seth yelling, "Dr. Kim, Dr. Kim, please come, please come!" I immediately got up and followed Seth to another hut, with my flashlight and textbooks in hand just in case I needed them for anything. I am glad I brought them, because I did need them. As I approached the hut, the scream got louder and louder, almost to the point that the noise was unbearable. Since the area had limited anesthesia, I was used to screaming while stitching or doing other procedures. But this woman was louder than anyone I had previously treated. When I finally arrived at the hut, I saw a woman getting ready to deliver a baby. After the initial shock I realized I knew nothing about delivering babies, so I immediately opened my book to find out how to. I skimmed very quickly because the screaming was getting to me, and I wanted to hurry. I had a general idea of how to deliver a baby but never delivered one so this was a new experience.

After reading—I mean skimming—the book, I told Seth to start a fire adjacent to me. He worked quickly and had a fire going in no time. I then told him to get a stone with a cutting edge, like the end of one of the arrows. He obliged me once again, bringing over several arrows. I told him to put the arrows in the small flame to sterilize them. He then asked why he should pass the arrows through the flame and what sterilization is. I explained to him about heating the arrows to kill bacteria and other pathogens to decrease the chance of infection. I don't think he knew what I was talking about, but he just said okay. I could also see that he wasn't paying too much attention to me and was concentrating on the woman. I laughed because he was about to pass out over the situation, but the woman's screams very quickly brought me back to reality. I know people over a one-half mile radius had to hear her. I had never heard anyone scream so loudly in my life.

After getting last-second notes from the books on cutting the cord, I instructed them to get me a cloth so I could wrap the baby up. Seth ran and got the cloth, and then he passed out from anxiety over the baby coming and running all over the village to get supplies. He was only out for a few seconds and before he was up again. I told him to stay there and relax because I didn't need anything else. If I did need anything, others could get it for me.

Back to the woman and the soon-to-be baby. While she was pushing and pushing, she grabbed her husband's hands and squeezed them until he was yelling too. I told him to try and be calm so that he didn't arouse her. He tried, but she squeezed very hard. I felt sorry for him because it looked like he was holding his breath so he wouldn't scream. As she pushed, she prayed out loud. That is one thing I noticed—all the people of the village were praying for a safe delivery and for me to have the courage and ability to deliver a healthy baby. I didn't realize this until later, but they blame the person who delivers the baby if there is a birth defect or any other complication. I am glad I didn't know this before I delivered, because that would have added stress. There were nurses watching me so I wasn't totally alone. They usually deliver them at the hospital so they know what to do. Remember they have been delivering babies forever so I wasn't needed. I just happened to be present.

As I sat waiting for the baby and encouraged her to push, I was about to be dazzled and amazed. I was going to find out what "the miracle of life" is all about. I was about to learn what it is like to bring a life into this world at its earliest stages. I was about to deliver a baby. By following the directions of the book, I had confidence that I could do everything correctly. I just hoped that there would not be any complications. I had no idea how much time had passed, but the moment was near. I first saw the head, and then the rest of the body came out. I then screamed, "*Vidzia le avi fam!*" which means, "The baby is crying!" I also screamed to the parents that the baby was a girl. I felt such joy, elation, and many inexplicable feelings. I just sat there and unable to believe that I had just brought a life into this world.

After reading on how to cut the umbilical cord, I brought the arrow out of the fire and cut it. I wrapped the baby in the cloth, cleaned off some of the fluids, and handed the baby to the mother. Since the baby was born on

Thursday, the mother said, "*Eyate nkenye nye Yao*," meaning the baby's Ghanaian name is Yao. After I handed the baby to her, she gave me a gift that I don't think I will get again for the rest of my life. She named her baby after me. She said, "We will name her Kim." I have never had such a gift or honor bestowed on me, and I don't think any honor I could receive could ever top this feeling. In Ghana, you receive two names, your Ghanaian name and also a western name.

Since most of the excitement was over, Seth finally got up and could deal with the newborn. He very comically said, "*Megafa fam avi o!*" which means, "Don't cry baby!" We all laughed, and the father led everyone in one last prayer. He thanked God for giving me the confidence and ability to deliver the baby and for giving them such a beautiful and healthy baby. Needless to say, I was on cloud nine for a few days. Before I left, I delivered around seven or eight babies, and each time was just as exhilarating as the first. Although no one else named a baby after me, I was thanked over and over. I hope to be able to deliver a baby again sometime in my life.

The injuries of the second patient that stands out in my mind resulted from lack of wildlife control. In an area where wildlife runs free, and there is no protection from the animals within the villages, there are going to be some incidents with the animals. The man that I had to treat was named John, and he had a run-in with the wildlife while hunting. He was about one-half of a mile from the hospital where I worked. Unfortunately, I didn't bring any books, except the drug book, to the hospital. I had to go to John without one. Others there told me that a crocodile took a big bite from his leg. I don't know what it was but it was a mess. So immediately I took a scalpel, some anesthesia (remember, they have anesthetics, but only a little bit to use on big cases, and I felt this was a big case), alcohol, painkillers, antibiotics, bandages, and some sutures.

I didn't have my book so I didn't really know how to handle the situation, but I had done so many sutures I thought I was capable of treating the patient. Suturing is the only way I knew how to fix and I didn't know if it would work. But since I had not seen the magnitude of the injury, I would not be able to tell if I could or could not do the job. I walked to the man and saw that the animal had ripped off half of the leg below the patella (the knee). It broke the bones completely, and the leg only hung on by the flesh of the skin. It was bleeding at a tremendous rate, and I had to do something. The lady delivering the baby was loud, but she was a mute compared to this guy. I immediately injected a local anesthesia into his leg. It did help some, but with the sheer amount of pain and the large area of injury, I didn't have enough. I first wrapped a cloth around his thigh to try and minimize the blood loss. I then gave him the painkillers from the dispensary (or pharmacy).

I had no idea what to do and didn't know how to save the leg, so I made the decision to amputate. I told him what I was about to do, and he said to hurry and to make the pain go away. I first cleaned the wound with alcohol. Then I took the scalpel and cut the remaining flesh attachment off, which was not much. He said he didn't feel it too much since I concentrated the anesthesia around the area where I was to cut. I then smoothed some of the sharp ends of the remaining bone structure. When I had cut the flesh and smoothed the sharp bone edges, I took the alcohol and cleaned the injury site again. There was a lot less blood than when I first arrived, but it was still flowing. I started to suture some of the larger cuts. I then took the excess flesh, flapped it over the entire area, and sutured the flap of flesh to the bottom of the limb. The sutures were self absorbent, so I didn't have to worry about retrieving them from under the flap of flesh. It took more than an hour to suture the entire flap, but I finally finished the suturing and cleaned the wound with alcohol one more time. After the last dose of alcohol, I wrapped it up with the bandages, and the other men carried him back to the village. Needless to say, he was still in pain. He was lucky that the government supplied alcohol, sutures, et cetera.

Thank goodness I had gloves in my pocket, because I would have been a little apprehensive about dealing with all the blood without them. I was soaked in blood, but it was just on my clothes. To my astonishment, the women got every bit of it out of my pants and shirt. I gave the man more pills to help minimize the throbbing pain. I couldn't give too many, because others would need the drugs, and I couldn't give them all to one person, no matter how much pain he was in.

After I had done my first and last major medical treatment, I felt that I could handle just about anything. I knew that wasn't true, but I think I dealt with the injury fairly well for having no real knowledge of how to perform such procedures. Even if I had known exactly what to do, I don't know if I could have done more. I was in the middle of nowhere with no instruments and limited supplies of anesthesia and drugs. After we got back to the hospital, John used the crutches that I had before they were taken apart, so the crutches did come in handy. They were a bit wobbly, but he didn't mind and was just glad he was able to use them to get around and was a little mobile. After a few days, he was doing well on the crutches, and he said that the pain wasn't too bad. I was glad that he was doing well and that the sutures were good enough to let his limb heal correctly. That was one of my biggest worries—that the sutures might come unraveled. My biggest concern after the treatment was infection—so I continued to watch him closely while I was there. Fortunately everything turned out okay, and when I left he was laughing and joking like he had before the incident. I hope he didn't get any infection.

These were the biggest cases that I dealt with, but I did treat many other injuries and sicknesses that were not quite as severe. I got a lot of practice suturing minor cuts and gashes before the animal incident. I also got to deal with snake and spider bites. A man working at the hospital got bit by a snake, but he didn't know if it was poisonous or not. I read about snake bites in the books that I brought and looked at the sections on how to treat them. The man said that it just hurt, and that nothing else was happening. I looked at the signs and symptoms of poisonous snake bites, and he didn't seem to exhibit any of them. Fortunately I must have diagnosed correctly, because he didn't have any problems after I treated the bite, so obviously not poisonous.

Another unique case was a patient who was a little boy. He and his friends were playing with arrows when one accidentally stuck in his left arm. I didn't know how to treat the problem, but I dealt with it in a way I thought would work. I gave him a local anesthesia, and then made small incisions to open the injury more so I could remove the arrow from the arm with minimal damage to the surrounding nerves and tissues. After I got the arrow out, I sutured him up and gave him some pain pills. I knew the anatomy and wasn't in danger of hitting the nerves or blood vessels. I gave pain pills and anesthesia to kids more frequently than adults because children don't deal with pain as well. Kids are also top priority, so no one cared if I gave medicine to the children first. Later, I checked up on him. His wound was healing nicely, but he didn't have any feeling in that area. A nerve was evidently cut in the area. I don't think it was a major nerve branching off the plexus, because he just lost feeling in that small area and not any major regions that the musculocutaneous, radial, ulnar, or other branches of the brachial plexus innervate. Aside from these injuries, I treated other conditions that require medication—malaria; tuberculosis; hypertension; molecular parasitic conditions, such as schismaniasis and leishmaniasis; and other diseases that don't require any suturing, anesthesia, or other minor surgery.

Pat: I took this picture after I had extracted her molar. It was very loose so she felt minimal pain. She is just now feeling where her tooth used to be.

Other cases that I treated were common viruses and diseases. The common cold and influenza were very prevalent. I also saw some strep throats and inflamed tonsils. Fever blisters, carbuncles, and toothaches were also very common to everyone. You can see a tooth extraction patient in my photo album. There were a few HIV and AIDS cases, but that disease wasn't common in that region of Ghana. There were a few cases, but not nearly as many as in other parts of Africa. If you recall, Ghana is a very religious country, so having multiple partners is rare. Marriage to one wife is a very common practice. I was told that the northern part of Ghana has a much higher rate of HIV and AIDS infection, because the people are not as conservative. They have multiple wives and multiple partners.

Aside from the rare tropical diseases, I also encountered the same injuries and diseases I would find at home. I knew that when I returned home I would have to get some tests done for some of the diseases I encountered. For instance, I would have to get a Purified Protein Derivative (P.P.D.) test, or a TB skin test. I would have to get others if I noticed any abnormalities to my body. I didn't want to take chances, so I determined that if I felt unusual when I got home I would get tested. I can say now that I have been home for awhile and gotten a TB test, and everything is okay. I haven't felt any discomforts, so I haven't needed any additional tests. I think the vaccinations I got before leaving helped tremendously, especially the larium, which is used against malaria, if you recall.

Although I have said many positive things about Ghana and Africa, I do have to mention one negative practice that takes place not only there, but in many other regions of Africa. In my opinion, this practice is not necessary and should be eliminated. Let me imprint a picture in your psyche of this serious and common practice.

"It's early in the morning and everyone is quiet. There is tension in the room where Susan, a five-year-old girl, lies on her back in the corner of the hut. Sandra, her aunt, watches in sadness as her niece undergoes a procedure now known as female genital mutilation (FGM), formerly called female circumcision." This procedure is very common and is completed without any form of anesthesia. Susan's external sexual organs are partially or totally cut away. Sandra doesn't approve but couldn't dissuade the mother or father from completing the process. She recalls her own experience going through this unusual ritual as a little girl. Living with this mutilation for the rest of her life is one of the major long-lasting effects of this practice. It is engraved in her memory forever. After the procedure is over, Sandra goes and gives support to the brave and confused little girl.

Let me give a brief synopsis of FGM. I will start by explaining the different types of mutilation—there are two. The first one is called Sunni, and the second form is called Pharaonic. Sunni is a more moderate form of FGM in which the covering of the clitoris is removed. Pharaonic involves the removal of the entire clitoris and the labia. The vulva is stitched together, leaving only a small hole for the elimination of urine and menstrual blood. As I have already mentioned, this practice is very common in the world today. A recent survey indicated that around one hundred million girls and women in more than thirty-five countries have been subjected to this mutilation. I have described the two different forms of mutilation, and I will now explain the reason why people perform this act. Female genital mutilation has been long performed to ensure chaste or monogamous behavior by suppressing female sexuality.

As with much of the health care in Third World countries, the knowledge required to do such procedures is lacking. Since cutting is necessary in FGM, many women die from this procedure. Death to the girls is usually caused by infections, but other problems may arise. Some other problems that can arise are trauma, bleeding, obstructed labor, difficult childbirth, and psychiatric problems that last for a lifetime. Although this practice is slowly changing, the older women are more resistant to the change because of the fear that men in the tribes won't want the women without the procedure. The younger generation is not instilled with these thoughts, so the move is gradual but significant. The population is slowly turning against FGM.

Although this practice is illegal in most if not all countries, it is still common. The police patrol is very active in Accra, as is evident by the tanks driving around the city and automatic weapons that the authorities carry. Outside the major cities of Accra or Kumasi, however, police protection is nonexistent. Anything could happen in the surrounding areas, as well as Anfoega, and government or police officials would have no knowledge of it. I have to say that even though the police squad is present in Accra, its function isn't quite known to me. The police do not enforce too much unless the national security is in danger. For example, if someone is violated in any way, such as robbery, they will normally not intervene. They let the people resolve such issues on their own. The police will get involved if someone takes a picture of the airport or other landmark building. They assume that people might sell these pictures or plan an attack with them. If they perceive the national security is in danger, there are stiff repercussions for such acts. Later in the book, you will find out how significant this is not only for the citizens of the area, but for me. I mention this problem in hopes of educating everyone about this serious practice of abuse to women. I hope with the curing agent of time and education this unnecessary ritual will be eradicated altogether.

Chapter 5

Coming Home

I have discussed a plethora of subjects and adventures ranging from the food to the people and the health care system. Female genital mutilation, my experience with patients, and President Clinton's visit to the country were also highlighted in the previous pages. As you might imagine, I will never forget my adventures in Ghana and the great continent of Africa, and I hope you won't forget it either. The people and the culture either met or exceeded all my expectations tenfold. Now that I have reached the conclusion of my trip, let me explain how and why I came home. As you have read, I had had a wild and crazy trip thus far, and I could add unusual. So should the story of my return home be any different? The answer is no. Let me start out by saying that I had to leave before my internship concluded.

I remember coming home from the hospital and being ready to rest. The long day of work and the long walk back to the hut were very difficult for me. As I neared the village, I noticed a lot of people walking around frantically. I started to wonder if someone was hurt or if maybe the chief had died. Those were the only possibilities I could think of that could cause such a stir. I stopped someone and asked what was wrong. The person didn't answer me and continued to run. I saw people collecting sticks and rocks. They usually gather sticks and rocks, but not in a frenzy.

When I finally reached the village, I saw the chief and didn't see anyone hurt. I became increasingly worried and scared. No one was calm, and no one would explain anything to me. I looked for Seth but couldn't find him anywhere. I was really getting scared and angry that no one would disclose any information to me. Seth soon arrived, and he sat me down. I asked him, "What is with the running and gathering of sticks and rocks?"

He looked and me and said, "Dr. Kim, there is going to be a war!"

I asked him to run that by me again.

He regurgitated the exact line, *"There is going to be a war!"*

I immediately became very scared and froze. I was sweating more than usual, and not just because of the inclement weather. I asked him why there was going to be a war. He told me that Sean, a tribe member, and Chris, a tribe member of the adjacent village, argued with each other. Apparently Chris told Sean that he lacked manhood. This, according to Seth, is enough to provoke a fight between tribes. I asked him what else had happened, thinking something this minute couldn't start a war. He told me that there was nothing else. Seth explained that Chris saying Sean lacked manhood implied that Sean's tribe lacked pride, respect, and manhood. Chris displayed a lack of respect for the tribe, and he also implied that the chief was not worthy of leading an entire village.

I soon realized that this was a country of great pride and respect. In the States some people think material items give one stature. Since there are few material items in that region of Ghana, pride and respect are the measuring sticks of status. Disrespect to anyone in any form is worthy of fighting. In America, it would not be a big deal for one person to say negative things, especially what Chris said to Sean. But in a country where pride and respect is so important, I began to understand why the little comment by Chris was so significant. Even now, I still can't believe anyone wanting to fight over such a comment, but I have to remind myself of their cultures and beliefs.

When I found out there was going to be a tribal war, I felt compelled to get my gluteus out of the area before it started. I asked Seth when he thought the fighting would occur, and he told me that they would fight in four days. I thought it was unusual that he knew the exact time so I asked him, "How do you know when the other tribe will attack?"

Seth told me he knew because of the "rules of war" in Ghana. I was shocked to hear that there were rules, and I asked him what kind of rules. He continued to tell me, "There are many rules in war." First, the two chiefs meet to decide on the day of the war. They also decide how long they will fight, whether it be one day or several days. All this information is decided when the chiefs meet. If it were any other time, I would think he was joking with me, but in this time of conflict, I knew Seth would not lie. He told me that the reason they have a time frame for the fighting is to limit the number of deaths. They know that the population isn't excessive and that the tribes can't afford to kill each other off. I could understand that logic. The second rule is that there are no sneak attacks. The element of surprise is absent in Ghanaian warfare, or at least in the area in which I stayed. Even though they will fight, both tribes have enough respect let the other prepare for the upcoming battle. I thought this was very unusual. Limiting the carnage is also a reason why sneak attacks aren't allowed.

The time between the chiefs' meeting and the actual fighting is a time when both sides prepare for battle. They do this either by making more bows and arrows or by making sharper stones. The time frame between the chiefs' meeting and the actual fighting is very critical for each tribe, and it is very important that the entire tribe work together on this cause. I thought it was very odd that both parties knew and followed these rules. I guess I was used to the wars from my history lessons, in which sneak attacks and decimation of the enemy led to victory. But among Ghanaian tribes, winning isn't the desired outcome as it is in modern-day warfare. The status of each village and each person is at stake.

The last rule that Seth told me is even more bizarre and interesting than the others. He said that Chris and Sean wouldn't fight in the war. The outcome of the battle would determine their fates. If Sean's village won, then he would live. And if Sean's village won, then obviously Chris's tribe would lose. This isn't too bizarre, but the hypothetical outcome of Chris's tribe losing wasn't normal at all. If Chris's tribe lost, he would have to die via castration. His own tribe would do the mutilation. The reason he would die is that with the loss of a war, a tribe loses status, pride, and respect. Since he brought those undesirable attributes to his tribe, Chris would have to die. If Sean's tribe won, he would have brought much pride, respect, and courage back to the village and would be praised. This scenario would also hold true if the roles were reversed. I couldn't believe one of the two was going to die. If I were either Sean or Chris, I would be petrified that my tribe would lose. I would also want to fight to save my own life, but that isn't allowed, as I already mentioned. After the battle, everything goes back to normal, and everyone gets along again. There are no grudges between the two tribes, so there is no prolonged warfare. I thought this was a very smart of each tribe so the killing wouldn't continue.

While Seth told me this information, he and I sharpened stones and rocks for battle. Other men were prepared the bows and arrows, while women prepared clay and clothing for battle. There was tension in the air because they all knew that loved ones were about to die. The chief told me that dying from natural causes is easier to handle than losing someone in a war. He said that he doesn't like war because of the lack of respect not only for others but for life. I asked him if I would be safe there while they fought. He told me there was no guarantee.

That prompted me to find a way out of the area before the four days had elapsed. I asked the chief for help. He told me the only way out was to pass the word along from tribe to tribe back to Accra. I knew that it took a three-hour car ride over about one hundred miles to get there. I thought I had better chances of finding a needle in a haystack than having my request reach Accra. But I tried it because it was the only option I had. I gave the adjacent tribe five thousand cedis and told them that I needed a taxi at this tribe. After giving them the money, I was very depressed because I didn't think I would ever get out of there. I knew I could get home when the program ended because Sandy and Paige were to come and get me. But since it wasn't the end of the program and traffic was nonexistent, a car was impossible to come by.

While I waited for the taxi to arrive, I helped the tribes-people make weapons and also helped the women prepare the attire the men were to wear. One unusual thing I noticed was that they didn't tell the children. The children continued to play around with no worries about the upcoming events. Concealing the war from the children is another piece of evidence that gave me the impression that they take great care of them. They treat them as if they were gold, and the kids take top priority in everything. If there is only a small portion of food gathered, the children get fed first, as I mentioned before. The Ghanaians know that children haven't experienced life, and since they value life so much, they protect them from everything they can to allow them to experience as much as they can. I think these are very admirable characteristics we should all strive for. I must say that in America, we do try to cherish and protect the children's lives as the Ghanaians do but I'm not sure if it is to the extent of the Ghanaian people.

After I had sent the word to the adjacent tribes to send a taxi, all I could do was sit and wait. The first day after requesting the taxi, I continued to sharpen rocks and stones for the tribe to use. During this troubling time, the villagers only hunted once a day. So if they didn't get anything on the one trip, there would be nothing to eat. The men hunted for food and only killed enough to feed the children, so the adults didn't eat that day. They did offer me some food, but I told them to give it to the children. I thought if they didn't eat, then I wouldn't either. We continued working nonstop, utilizing all the daylight available.

When the first day of waiting was over, the second day soon came. Early in the morning they held a ritual tribal dance. Remember that tribal dances aren't just for religious purposes. They practiced techniques for uniformity and discipline during warfare. The dancing is similar to the cadences that our military follows. It helps make sure that everyone is on the same page and following uniformity and order. After working several hours, the men went hunting again and caught nothing for the second consecutive day. By this time, I was starting to get a little desperate for food, but not too desperate. When two days had passed, I thought my original belief I was wasting time and energy in asking for a taxi was coming true. I still had a little faith left, but it was disappearing with every hour that passed.

The third day came and it was the evening before the war. I was really starting to get nervous. My hope and faith was hanging on by the thread of a needle. My want for food was turning into need. I was very weak and needed something to eat very soon. Even though the entire tribe hadn't eaten, we all continued to work. Seth told me to eat leaves and small insects, which he had been telling me to do since the first day of the food drought. But I couldn't. I had eaten some weird delicacies but wasn't about to eat leaves and small insects. Others ate them to maintain their strength and energy. I obviously lacked both, so Seth once again told me to eat what was available.

The third day's hunt only generated enough for the children. This drought was caused by hunting only once a day and shortening the hunt by half. When the conclusion of the third day approached, I was very hungry. I had become desperate and finally gave in to eating some of the foods that Seth suggested. I grabbed leaves that I saw them eat and began to eat them as well. I hate to admit this, but I did venture to eat a small insect. You have to remember how desperate I was, and when there is no food, one will eat anything. And I did—I had grasshoppers. I saw Seth and the other tribespeople eat them, and I couldn't bring myself to eat a live one. I didn't think I would ever eat such precarious edibles, but I think anyone pushed to the limit will do just about anything. I didn't eat many grasshoppers, but I did eat one. I mostly filled up on leaves. I will also add that my gastrointestinal tract wasn't in the best condition for the evening. I took Immodium, and that alleviated much of the problem. I was totally sure that I wasn't going home and that I would have to stay for the war. I think my sick feeling was from the thought of eating the grasshopper more than getting sick from the food.

One might expect that we produced a lot of weapons with so many men working so many hours. But with the labor and the manpower, we did not produce much at all. The pile of weapons looked as if it came from a day's work, not three.

It was getting dark, and my hopes and dreams of getting out had emaciated. I couldn't believe that I was going to be there for a war and afraid that I wouldn't make it home. I had had my bags packed since the first day I knew that there was to be a war, so I was ready to go. But I still had no ride out of Anfoega. I never slept one wink that night and kept thinking of every possible negative outcome for the next day's events. Seth told me they were to meet at nine o'clock in the morning. I wished him and his family good luck and prayed that they survived the conflict. Time seemed to move like malaccas, or turtles, or any other clichés one can think of. That was the longest night in my life. I reflected on my entire life—my family, my friends, school, and the new friends and experiences I had gained in Africa.

As I heard the drums, I heard a horn. I immediately rose and yelled for the combatants to wait. Seth grabbed my bags and took them to the taxi. I said my good-byes and wished them all the best. I gave Seth my address so he could write and tell me if everything was okay. I got into the car and knew that I would be alright. As we were pulling away, I heard Seth yelling and running toward the car. He told me that he would come with me to make sure that I could leave without any problems. I would normally have said that I would be alright, but I didn't because I knew if he were with me that he wouldn't die in the conflict. I can't explain my feelings, but I was both elated and sad as we pulled away from the village. I was happy that I wouldn't be around for the conflict but also sad that I would never see those fine people again. As we drove farther away, I looked back and waved to the villagers. They all waved back and cried. With this internship, I had just experienced something rare and unique with some of the greatest people I ever knew. These emotions and the waving and crying villagers brought a tear to my eye as well.

The three-hour ride back to Accra was very quiet because we were both sad that I had to leave. When we got there, it was around eleven o'clock in the morning and I immediately went to the airport to change my ticket. Remembering the hassle that I had to endure upon my arrival in Ghana, I knew not to let anyone help me or I would have to tip. After changing my ticket information, I had six hours before I had to leave, so we went to get something to eat. And believe me, since this was the first meal I had had in more than three days, I stuffed myself.

Seth also took me shopping for souvenirs. I bought an African guitar and a wooden symbol called, *"Gye nayme!"*

which means, "Only God!" I also bought a ring, *kente* clothing, purses, necklaces, jewelry for my nieces, and a vase for my sister. My "art of negotiation" came in handy once again when shopping. I negotiated with all of the dealers to get the best prices. I also bought two authentic *kente* outfits for my parents. I knew that they would never

Kudzo: he is the man that made the vase that I purchased for my sister. He made it in that dome. I walked in it and it was very hot. He let me take this picture with the stipulation that I have to mail him back a copy. FYI, I did mail him back this picture as I promised.

wear them, but I thought they would make unique gifts and be very nice to have.

When I had bought some gifts for my family and filled my stomach, I was ready to head home. I had an hour and a half until the flight was to leave, so we headed back to the airport. I wanted to make sure I had enough time to board in case I had complications from the converted ticket. As the taxi drove up to the airport, Seth started to cry. He got out of the car and got my luggage, and we entered the airport check-in desk. For security reasons, this was as far as Seth was permitted to go unless he was going to fly. When I was ready to enter the terminal, Seth started to cry again. He told me that I was the best thing that had happened to him and his tribe—because I volunteered and gave the tribe things, and because I was such a good friend. I told him how much I valued our friendship and that I hoped we could write to each other. We exchanged addresses again, and we both said good-bye. As I entered the terminal, I looked back and waved, and he was waving back.

On my way back home, I traveled the same route as I had in coming to Ghana. I stopped in Amsterdam again. Since I couldn't find a phone in Ghana, I had to call home to tell my parents that I was coming home early. When my mother answered the phone, she started to ask questions about my trip. I told her that things were going well and that I was in Amsterdam.

She said, "Where, what, why?"

I told her that I would be back home the next evening.

She was very worried and asked again, "Why?"

I told her that there was a tribal war, and that I wanted to leave before it got worse. She and my father were both frantic, but I told them that I was out of danger and in Amsterdam. That calmed them down, and then we had a civil conversation. After explaining to them what time I would arrive, they tried to ask me more questions, but I told them I would explain when I got home. I knew that they were dying to hear about some of the adventures I had, and I couldn't wait to tell them. I also knew that my stories were well worth telling and I think well worth listening to—or in this case reading about. After the six-hour delay in Amsterdam, I got on the plane that was to head back to the States.

After arriving in Columbus, my parents and my cousin Christopher were waiting for me. They saw me carrying my backpack with my sister's vase and the drum that I had made. After saying hello, we started to walk to the baggage claim. While we were walking, my father stopped, looked at me, and asked, "Where are your crutches?" I told him the story of the tribespeople taking them apart and that I had just given the crutches to them. He and my mother laughed. I think they were a little worried about being around me for fear of the microorganisms that I could have brought back. I thought it was funny.

As we waited for the luggage, I told them some of the stories, and they were in disbelief. They said that they could not have lived like that, even for a day. I told them I didn't think I could either, but I did. After we waited for ten minutes, my luggage never came. It was no surprise that I had trouble with my luggage—it was just indicative of my entire trip. I was afraid that it was in Amsterdam. The airline clerk said that another plane was to arrive from Philadelphia, and there was a good chance that my luggage was on it. So we went to eat while we waited for the luggage to arrive. The first thing I ate was spaghetti, my favorite meal. While we ate I told them more stories and more stories. They were engrossed in the tales of my adventures, and I could not blame them. I had a very unique trip.

After eating we went back to the airport, and my luggage was there. On the way home, my father said, "From your experiences, I bet you will never want to do that again." He, my mother, and my cousin were surprised to hear that I loved the entire trip and would do it again in a heartbeat. They said, "You would?" I told them that this made me want to do missionary work even more in the less-developed countries. They thought this trip would make me never want to volunteer in a Third World country again. They were wrong—this trip increased my desire to volunteer and help those less fortunate.

In fact, when I get out of school, I want to make regular trips to different parts of the world to give free health care to those that need it the most. I hope I am fortunate enough to do such work. I know of many health providers that send volunteers yearly to less-developed countries. Knowing that it is possible through my experiences in Ghana, I will one day go throughout the world to help others. My friend from Louisville, Amy Young, concurs with me and wants to volunteer together regularly after establishing our respective practices. We talked on the phone for hours about our adventures and how we both enjoyed Africa. She loved her experience as much as I loved mine. In fact, we both wrote to each other via post-cards while we were there.

Her stories were just as full of adventure as mine. She told me about her safari. Tourists were sitting on the bus, and suddenly a rhino ran at it and hit the side right next to Amy. She was thankful that there were bars across the windows and the side of the bus, because they protected her and the other people from injury. After the rhino hit the bus, it ran away and didn't bother them again. Glass was all over the place, but everyone was okay. She and I couldn't wait to look at each other's photo albums. I am sad that I didn't get any pictures of the living conditions, but I think I got some good pictures of how the Ghanaians live. She has many more stories, but that is another book. From my stories of Ghana and her story of Kenya, you can see Africa is full of adventures and new and great experiences for all of us.

Branded into my mind are the smiling, happy children; the elegant, dignified women; and the courageous, hard-working men. The adventures that I have been fortunate to experience come once in a lifetime. The kindness, the sharing, the unselfishness, and the industriousness all have a unique place in my life. Seth, the chief, and everyone else will always be a big part of my life. I hope one day that I can go back and see some of the same people. I suggest to those who have adventurous spirits, go to Africa. It is truly a beautiful and wonderful continent. The landscape, as well as the people, culture, and beliefs, are all beautiful.

I have learned so much and know that these experiences have made me into a more learned and better individual. Among the things I have learned are to be more open-minded toward other cultures and to give them a chance. I should not be judgmental without giving others a chance. I also learned to appreciate what I have and not to complain about what I do not have. The biggest and most important thing I learned on this trip is that one does not have to have everything or even have anything in this crazy world in order to be happy. Seeing those people in Anfoega and the hospital smiling, laughing, and being happy without anything epitomizes true happiness to me. I am glad that I could witness such pure and happy lifestyles.

I have many memories of Ghana, but none will be more prevalent than that of the person that I value meeting the most—Seth. He was invaluable during my entire stay in Ghana. He is one of the kindest, nicest persons I have ever known. He exhibits many good qualities, and he will help anyone, any time. Without him I would not have had anywhere to live. He also stayed with me until I left. He was a great friend, and I hope that he will make it to the States one day. I will add now that since I have returned from Africa, he has written to me twice. He made me laugh—some of the items I gave him before I left have made him one of the most popular people in his community. He also told me that the pictures and the cassette tape of American music I gave him were great. The hospital employees loved them also and, they were glad I kept my word that I would send the pictures back to them. He told me that he goes to Accra and listens to the tape all the time. He wrote that he was glad that I left because the hut was destroyed, and that would have been where I would have waited for the battle to conclude. It would have meant danger for me, so I was also relieved that I retreated before the conflict began. Seth is still working at the hospital.

Besides sending two letters, Seth also called me from Accra and told me he used the money I gave him to buy time at the communication center. I gave him some Ghanaian money since I didn't have time to exchange it for U.S. dollars. He told me that many people died in the conflict, including some of his closest friends. He was saddened but said that the tribes are fine and getting along. I was glad that nothing happened to him. Seth taught me so much about African culture and his way of life without ever being offended by my questions, no matter how ridiculous they were. I would like for him to come to the States and let me show him and tell him about our culture. I know how badly he wants to see what America is like, and there is no other person that I can think of who would make the most of his stay. I will always value his friendship and want to thank him for his help during my visit.

In conclusion, I would like to thank you for reading my stories about this trip in the summer of 1998—the summer of '98 is a summer I will not soon forget. The language, rituals, and most of all the people, will forever remain a major chapter in my life. I still can't believe the richness of Ghana and Africa in everything one could ever imagine, and I would encourage everyone to go visit sometime in his or her life. From my trip, I can honestly say that Africa is truly a magnificent and mysterious continent, and I am glad that I can share it with you. I am sure my friend Amy, and anyone else that has ever visited or lived in Africa, knows exactly what I am talking about. I really that hope you enjoyed my stories and learned a few things along the way. If you did, then I fulfilled my goal. So if you accidentally learned something and mistakenly enjoyed the book, thank you. I know I enjoyed the trip and telling you about it. When I was writing this book and submitting it for publication, I knew even if my manuscript wasn't accepted for publication, I would have a great record of this amazing trip. Obviously, I was fortunate to get it published but more importantly, I have the book to bring back some great memories.